Listen & Perform
The TPR Student Book
For Beginning and Intermediate ESL Students

by
Stephen Mark Silvers

edited by
James J. Asher

First Edition
ISBN 0-940296-29-2
First Printing 1985

Second Edition
ISBN 1-56018-486-5
First Printing 1994

D1736760

published by
Sky Oaks Productions, Inc.
P.O. Box 1102 • Los Gatos, CA 95031
Phone: (408) 395-7600 • **Fax:** (408) 395-8440

TABLE OF CONTENTS

To The Teacher

Listen and Perform provides a stress-free introduction to English for ESL students using the Total Physical Response (TPR) approach originated by Professor James J. Asher of San Jose State University in San Jose, California.

The Total Physical Response approach recreates, to a large extent, the process that a child uses to acquire its first language. In the book, **Learning Another Language Through Actions** (4th Edition), Dr. Asher cites the following three elements of child language acquisition which form the basis for the TPR approach:

   a. The infant develops a high level of listening competency **before** the child begins to speak. A child whose production is limited to one or two-word utterances is perfectly capable of understanding a complex sentence such as "Go into your room and get your ball." The child cannot yet produce this sentence but demonstrates understanding by performing the action.

   b. There is an intimate relationship between language and a child's body. Much of the child's first exposure to language comes in the form of commands given by an adult or "caretaker" to guide the child in relation to concrete objects and actions as for example:

> Hold my hand.
> Pick up your truck.
> Don't go near the stove. It's hot.

   c. The child speaks when the individual is **ready.** Just as a parent cannot teach an infant to walk, one cannot teach an infant to talk. The infant begins to talk when a stage of readiness is reached, and this **"readiness"** is contingent upon first having assimilated a good portion of the language code. Speech cannot be taught; it is a developmental process which will appear spontaneously when the child is **ready to speak.**

Dr. Asher hypothesizes that people are biologically programmed for language acquisition and that this acquisition takes place in a particular sequence. He states that

> "A reasonable hypothesis is that the brain and nervous system are biologically programmed to acquire language, either the

first or second, in a particular sequence and in a particular mode. The sequence is listening before speaking and the mode is to synchronize language with the individual's body." (Asher, 1983).

Based on these observations of how a child acquires its first language, Dr. Asher has devised an instructional strategy that he first introduced more than 20 years ago as the "Total Physical Response." In this approach, initially the students do not speak but silently act out commands given by the teacher. These commands begin with simple phrases such as "Walk to the door," but can soon be expanded in length and complexity to "Walk to the student who's wearing a yellow blouse and give her the flower that's on the floor next to the desk." As the students listen to the teacher and perform the commands (the total physical response) they build up a cognitive map of the language. When the students have internalized a sufficient part of the language code, like the child learning its first language, they reach a stage of **readiness to speak**. At this point, the roles are reversed and the students are invited to give the commands to their teacher and classmates.

In our work over the last six years teaching English to students in Brazil from elementary school, high school and the University of the Amazons, we have observed the following **postive features** of a TPR approach with beginning ESL students:

- The use of **real objects and actions** in the classroom makes the language concepts more concrete and easier to grasp.

- The **total involvement** of the student's body in performing the actions speeds up the linking of meaning to the sounds heard and facilitates assimilation of the new language code.

- The use of the muscular-motor system aids in producing not only short-term retention, but more importantly **long-term retention**.

- Responding physically rather than verbally **eliminates the students' fear of speaking** incorrectly and appearing foolish in front of their classmates.

- The class can be given in English with perfect comprehension, starting with the very first session, **eliminating the need to translate** into the students' native language.

- As the students mentally process the teacher's commands, associating the actions with the spoken words, they **learn to think in English.**

2

- The fast-moving pace, the variety of the commands, and the feeling of success that the students experience all help maintain a **high level of student motivation.**

- This approach is well-suited to multi-level classes in which you find true beginners along with false beginners and intermediate level students.

Listen and Perform provides material for 75 to 100 hours of classroom instruction, and could be used in any of the following situations:

a. As an **introductory English course,** after which the students would continue their studies using another language series, but at an accelerated pace due to their high level of comprehension.

b. As an **elective listening comprehension course** offered concurrently with the regular English course.

c. As a **supplement to a regular English course,** in which part of each class would be devoted to TPR activities. Used in this manner, **Listen and Perform** provides supplementary material for four semesters of English study.

d. As a **combination introductory course/supplement.** For the first 30 to 40 hours of instruction, only **Listen and Perform** would be used. Then the students would switch to another language series but would continue using **Listen and Perform** on a regular basis as a supplement.

e. As a **self-study book for students** who have some knowledge of English but who don't have time to study in a formal language class. Since the Key Sentences are illustrated, the student can listen to the tape and perform the actions in the pictures.

Suggestions for the teaching of **Listen and Perform** may be found in my **Teacher's Guidebook** which can be ordered from Sky Oaks Productions, Inc. Incidentally, if you are new to TPR, I highly recommend that you start with these two practical, easy-to-read books:

Learning Another Language Through Actions by James J. Asher.
and
Instructor's Notebook: How To Apply TPR For Best Results by Ramiro Garcia.

Then follow up by viewing one or more of the classic video demonstrations showing the effectiveness of TPR in helping children and adults acquire many different languages. A complete description of the books and videos may be found in the back of this book under **TPR Products.** Here are the *video titles:*

Children Learning Another Language: An Innovative Approach
A Motivational Strategy for Language Learning
Strategy for Second Language Learning
Demonstration of a New Strategy in Language Learning

3

The Total Physical Response approach to language teaching has been documented by more than twenty years of research. The following articles describe in detail much of the research and will provide further insights regarding the theoretical and practical applications of the TPR model:

Asher, J.J. "The total physical response approach to second language learning." **The Modern Language Journal,** 1969, 53 (1) 3-17.

Asher, J.J. "Children's first language as a model for second language learning." **The Modern Language Journal,** 1972, 56 (3) 133-139.

Asher, J. J. "Children learning another language: a developmental hypothesis." **Child development,** 1977, 48, 1040-1048.

Asher, J. J. "Motivating children and adults to acquire a second language." **SPEAQ Journal,** 1979, Vol. 3, Nos. 3-4, 87-99.

Asher, J.J. "Fear of foreign languages." **Psychology Today,** August 1981, 52-59.

Asher, J. J. "Comprehension training: The evidence from laboratory and classroom studies." In **The Comprehension Approach to Foreign Language Instruction.** H. Winitz (ed.) Rowley, MA: Newbury House Publishers, Inc., 1981.

Asher, J. J. "The extinction of second language learning in American schools: An intervention Model." In **The Comprehension Approach to Foreign Language Instruction.** H. Winitz (ed.) Rowley, MA: Newbury House Publishers, Inc., 1981.

Asher, J. J. "The total physial response: Theory and practice." In **Native Language and Foreign Language Acquisition.** H. Winitz (ed.) Vol. 379, 324-331. **The Annals of the New York Academy of Sciences,** 1981.

Finally, it is important that the students understand how to use **Listen and perform,** which is why I have written the next section entitled, **To The Student.** If you speak the students' native language, you should translate this introduction and go over it with them in class, making sure they understand how to use the book. This may be impossible if several languages are spoken in your class. However, most students will have a friend or relative who speaks English and who could translate for them.

Hint to the Instructor

Before the student can successfully work in this TPR student workbook, the assumption is that **Lessons 1 through 10** have been thoroughly internalized in many hours of TPR classroom instruction.

TPR instruction in the classroom works like this: At the front of the class, with a student seated on either side of you, you say, "Stand up" and you along with your students then stand up. Next you say, "Sit down," and you with your students, sit down. This is called **modeling.** In modeling, you are communicating meaning when you utter a direction in the target language, then perform the appropriate behavior.

After several demonstrations of **stand up** and **sit down,** next model **walk, stop, turn,** and **jump.** When the audience has observed you and the students on either side of you act in response to commands, the observers are also internalizing the meaning of the spoken language.

After modeling a sequence such as, stand up, walk, stop, etc., for a number of times, the students become ready to act **alone** without you. At this point, you invite an individual student who was performing with you to try it alone. You utter a direction such as, stand up, and the individual student acts alone in response to each command.

Once students are responding rapidly and with confidence to a sequence of commands, **model** again with expansions of the commands such as, "Walk to the chair," "Walk to the door," and "Walk to the sofa."

As students become more and more comfortable and confident that they understand everything you are saying in the target language, then recombine constituents to create **novel** directions—ones the students have never heard before but understand perfectly. For example, the students have experienced:

Walk to the door. Touch the door. Walk to the chalkboard. Now, will they understand if you recombine elements to create a **novel sentence** such as: Touch the chalkboard.

Recombining elements to create novel sentences is, as Asher (1983) has stated,". . . the essence of fluency" because it helps students achieve flexibility of thinking in the target language.

After students are responding rapidly and confidently to any direction from lessons 1 through 10, they are **ready** to enjoy this TPR student workbook. At this point, students are ready to see the English in print and, starting with lesson 1, begin TPR exercises in reading and writing.

To The Student

Listen and Perform is based on what we could call a "natural" method of language learning. We say that it is a "natural" method because it follows the same procedure an infant uses to learn its first language. Most of us have amnesia for our infancy, but if you observe babies, you will notice these curious events:

a. For the first year or so **the baby is silent** except for babbling. During this pre-speaking stage, the baby's brain is working to decipher the language code, trying to make sense from the sounds it hears, and sorting those sounds into meaningful patterns.

b. The baby understands much, much more than it can speak. If you say, "Go into your room and get your ball" to a two year old, the child will walk into the room and get the ball; but the baby could never produce that sentence. Before a baby can produce even a simple four word sentence such as "Give me the ball," there first must be a sophisticated understanding of the spoken language. **Listening competency develops well in advance of speaking.**

c. The baby demonstrates understanding by physical actions, not by speaking. Much of what the baby hears during the first two years is in the form of gentle commands used to direct the infant's behavior in relation to concrete objects and actions, such as

> Give me your hand.
> Put on your shoes.
> Don't touch the stove. It's hot.

In this course, you will follow the same steps as the baby. For the first 10 to 15 hours **you will not speak** but will **perform commands** given by the teacher. During this time, you will be assimilating vocabulary and language structures. When you have internalized enough of the language code, **you will be ready to speak.** Then the roles will be reversed, and you will give commands to your teacher and classmates.

You may wonder how you are going to learn the grammar of English. **Listen and Perform** presents most of the basic structures of English through commands called **Key Sentences.** If, at the end of this course, you can perform and speak these commands without hesitation, you will have assimilated the grammar without any conscious effort.

How to Use Listen and Perform

The primary objectives of **Listen and Perform** are first, to develop a high level of competency in **understanding** the spoken language, and secondly, to develop **fluency of expression**. The exercises in this book are designed to provide training in both the listening and speaking skills, with primary emphasis on listening. Practice is also given in reading and writing English.

The **Key Sentences, Participation Exercises and Visual Practice Exercises** are all based on commands which can easily be performed in the classroom and at home. These commands are the backbone of **Listen and Perform** and to obtain the maximum benefit from this course you must practice the commands by **actually performing them**, either listening to the tape or working with a friend. It is not sufficient to just read or write the commands; you must actively participate, experience the commands with a **total physical involvement of your whole body.** Furthermore, do not practice the commands one time and feel that you have learned them. **The commands should be practiced until you can perform them easily and without hesitation.**

You should frequently review the commands from previous lessons. If you conscientiously practice the commands in this manner, actually performing them, you will soon develop a high level of listening competency, which in turn will lead to fluency of expression. Below are some suggestions on how to study the different sections of **Listen and Perform.**

Key Sentences

- Listen to the tape (or a friend) and perform the actions.

- Read the commands for a friend to perform.

- Cover the commands, look at your drawings, and give the commands for a friend to perform.

- Cover the commands, look at your drawings, and write the commands.

- Close the book, listen to the tape (or a friend) and write the commands.

Participation Exercises

- Listen to the tape (or a friend) and perform the actions.

- Read the commands for a friend to perform.

7

Visual Practice Exercises

- Listen to the tape (or a friend) and perform the actions.

- Give the commands for a friend to perform.

- Listen to the tape (or a friend) and answer the questions.

- Work with a friend, asking and answering questions about your drawings.

Pronunciation Exercises

- Listen to the tape (or a friend) and perform the actions.

- Give the commands for a friend to perform.

Review and Reinforcement

- Do not just write the answers. Copy and write the complete sentences.

- After you have done the exercises, check your answers in the **Key to the Exercises**, pages 178 to 184.

- Correct your mistakes.

For the best use of **Listen and Perform,** please remember the following:

— Study by **performing the commands**. This is the key to the successful use of **Listen and Perform.**

— **Do not practice speaking** until you have completed lesson 10 and have experienced the role reversal training in the classroom.

— Practice speaking only the commands that you can listen to and perform without hesitation.

— Study with a friend, preferably a friend who has some knowledge of English.

— Frequently review the commands and exercises from past lessons.

— Avoid translation. Usually the meaning will be clear from the teachers demonstration and from your drawings.

Assembling the Materials

In order to use **Listen and Perform** correctly you will first have to assemble the following objects, most of which are easily available in your own home, at the supermarket, or in a toy store. You should keep these objects in a box or a bag so that they will always be ready for your practice. As you obtain each item, check it off on the list below.

_____ bag	_____ glass
_____ ball	_____ glasses
_____ bell	_____ hat
_____ book	_____ key
_____ bottle	_____ magazine
_____ bottle caps	_____ matches
_____ bowl	_____ necklace
_____ box	_____ newspaper
_____ bracelet	_____ pail
_____ can	_____ pen
_____ candle	_____ pencil
_____ coin	_____ pitcher
_____ comic book	_____ ring
_____ crown	_____ scissors
_____ cup	_____ sponge
_____ eraser	_____ tie
_____ earring	_____ towel
_____ flower	_____ watch

_____ geometric figures (simple set)

_____ geometric figures (double set)

The following objects are probably best obtained as inexpensive children's toys:

ball, bracelet, earring, glasses, hat, necklace, pail, scissors, watch, wig

9

Other objects can be made by cutting them out of stiff construction paper:

crown, tie, geometric figures

You will need two sets of geometric figures.

Set A (simple set — one of each figure)

Set B (double set — two of each figure)

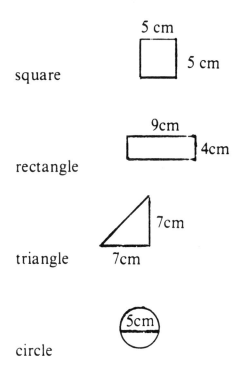

square

rectangle

triangle

circle

Some of the objects need a little explanation such as:

bottle — plastic, liquid detergent bottle or similar.

bottle caps — You will need about 10. Keep them in a can.

box — shoe box, toothpaste box.

can — use a can with a lid, powdered milk can or — similar.

flower — plastic

hat — could be made of stiff construction paper.

matches — use box matches.

tie — make one from heavy construction paper.

Important Reminder to the Instructor from the Editor

Before your students begin the exercises in this workbook, they will have internalized, by following your directions in the classroom, the content in the **Participation Exercises** from Lessons 1 through 10.

For example, before your students are given this workbook, you will ask a student to sit on either side of you at the front of the class. Then you say, "stand, " and you stand up along with the students who are sitting next to you. Then you say, "sit down," and you sit down along with the students. **This is modeling.** The students in the class listen to your one-word direction in the target language and they observe the action that follows each direction.

With a student on either side of you, model: stand up, sit down, stand up, sit down, stand up, walk, stop, walk, stop, walk, stop, turn, turn, walk, stop, turn, sit down.

Then a student who is sitting next to you is invited to **try it alone.** You may say, "Maria, stand up. Sit down, stand up, walk, stop, walk, stop, turn, turn, walk," etc.

After this, other students are invited to perform all by themselves. You, of course, demonstrate if an individual is hesitant. The objective is to **build student confidence,** not to trick or embarrass them.

When students are responding rapidly and with confidence to one-word directions, then expand with "Walk to the chair. Touch the chair. Walk to the door. Touch the door. Walk to the sofa. Touch the sofa." etc. Of course, you model each new direction first for several times before students are invited to perform alone. You continue with other directions in the **Participation Exercises** that are in each lesson.

For many class meetings before students ever see the **Listen and Perform** workbook, they are listening to directions and acting. During this time they are internalizing and understanding a large sample of the target language that is in the **Participation Exercises.** They are sorting out the patterns of the new language and becoming comfortable with the strange phonology of the new language.

When the students have internalized listening comprehension for the content in about ten lessons of the **Participation Exercises,** then most will be ready to start with the **Listen and Perform** workbook. They will be ready to work through each exercise starting with Lesson 1.

You continue to help students in the classroom expand their compre-

Important Reminder to the Instructor from the Editor(Cont.)

hension through TPR instruction which is: utter a new direction, model the new direction several times, then students try it alone, but now for a portion of the class session, students can work alone or with partners on exercises that you assign in the workbook.

In summary, the students' listening comprehension of the target language will be far in advance of their reading and writing because they will **understand** the spoken language through Lesson 10, but will begin in the **Listen and Perform** workbook at Lesson 1.

You will introduce new directions in class from Lesson 11, while students are working alone or with a partner on Lesson 2 in the workbook. This procedure increases the chances for a graceful, stress-free transition from listening comprehension which is **the primary skill** to ancillary skills of reading, writing, and speaking.

Incidentally, as you work with students to expand their listening comprehension with TPR instruction, please keep in mind a rule-of-thumb by Gene Lynch, a TPR instructor of high school German in Lompoc, California. The Lynch rule is to review all the TPR content from yesterday and half of the content from the day before yesterday. The other rule-of-thumb by James Asher is to relax, take your time, move in a gentle step-by-step development and enjoy the sensational results along with your students.

LESSON ONE

You Will Need

chair   sofa   television

Key Sentences

Draw a picture to illustrate each Key Sentence.

1. Stand up and jump. **(Sample)**

2. Walk to the door.

3. Now jump to the sofa.

4. Touch the television.

5. Walk to the chair and sit down.

6. Walk, stop, turn around and jump.

7. Jump to the window and touch it.

8. Walk to a friend and touch him.

9. Walk to a friend and touch her.

10. Whisper "good-bye" to a friend.

11. Wave to a friend.

12. Jump to a friend and say "Touch me".

13. Shake hands with a friend.

14. Touch the chalkboard.

15. Everybody stand up.

16. Say "hello" to the teacher.

17. Don't sit down.

18. Now sit down.

Participation Exercises

1.

Stand up
Walk
Stop
Jump
Turn Around
Sit down

2. Walk to the

chair
door
sofa
television
window

3. Jump to the

window
door
chair
sofa
television

4. Touch the

window
television
sofa
door
chair

5.

Walk Jump	to me and	touch me
		shake hands with me
		say "hello" to me
		whisper "good-bye" to me

6.

Walk Jump	to a friend and	touch her
		wave to her
		say "hello" to her
		shake hands with her

7.

Walk Jump	to a friend and	touch him
		wave to him
		shake hands with him

14

Review and Reinforcement

Excercise 1

Copy the sentence below, filling in each blank with the appropriate word.

1. Shake _____ with a friend. (window   hands   door)

2. _____ to the door. (jump   stand   whisper)

3. Touch _____ window. (the   up   and)

4. _____ to a friend. (touch   hello   wave)

5. Everybody sit _____ . (chair   say   down)

6. Say "hello" _____ me. (to   now   chalkboard)

7. Walk to the chair and touch _____ . (him   her   it)

8. Jump to the sofa _____ a friend. (sit   with   around)

9. Walk to John and touch _____ . (him   friend   chair)

10. Stand up and _____ around. (touch   turn   whisper)

Exercise 2

Reorder the words below to form correct sentences.

1. chalkboard touch the (**Sample**) Touch the chalkboard.

2. stand everybody up

3. to sofa jump the

4. me say "hello" to

5. the walk window to

6. a friend to wave

7. the whisper to "good-bye" teacher

8. hands with shake friend a

9. walk down sofa and sit the to

10. it and window to jump the touch

15

Lesson Summary

A	indefinite article **a**	Wave to **a** friend.
B	definite article **the**	Walk to **the** door.
C	indefinite pronoun **everybody**	**Everybody** stand up.
D	conjunction **and**	Stand up **and** jump.
E	prepositions **to, with**	Jump **to** the chalkboard. Shake hands **with** a friend.
F	negative imperative	**Don't** sit down.

G object pronouns (partial list)

Walk to	Maria Pedro me the sofa	and touch	**her** **him** **me** **it**

H contraction

don't = do + not

Vocabulary

a	him	teacher
and	it	television
chair	jump	the
chalkboard	me	to
don't	now	touch
door	say	turn around
everybody	shake hands	walk
friend	sit down	wave
good-bye	sofa	whisper
hello	stand up	window
her	stop	with

LESSON TWO

You will need

chair   desk   fan   sofa   table   television

Key Sentences

Draw a picture to illustrate each Key Sentence.

1. Swim around the table. **(Sample)**

2. Run to the fan.

3. Walk around the room.

4. Hop to a wall.

5. Sit on the floor.

6. Hop to the table

7. Point to the ceiling.

8. Change places with a friend.

9. Jump around the class.

10. Touch the desk.

11. Jump to the door. Then point to the floor.

12. Shake hands with every student in the class.

13. If I point to the floor, jump. But if I point to the ceiling, hop.

Participation Exercises

1. Walk to the

table
fan
sofa
wall
door

2. Hop to the

wall
table
fan
televison
chair

3. Run to the

wall
door
window
sofa

4. Swim to the

fan
door
wail
chair
television

5.

Jump
Hop
Walk
Run
Swim

around the chair

6. Walk

to
around

the

table
chair
sofa
fan

18

7.   Point to the

| ceiling |
| floor |
| fan |
| table |
| window |

8.   Sit on the

| sofa |
| chair |
| floor |
| table |
| desk |

Review and Reinforcement

Exercise 1

Copy the sentences below, filling in each blank with a word.

1. Jump _____ the class. (now   on   around)
   (Sample) Jump around the class.

2. Point to the _____ . (ceiling   wave   who)

3. Walk to the chalkboard. _____ sit down. (then   that   eyes)

4. Change _____ with the teacher. (walls   places   hands)

5. _____ to a friend. (table   desk   hop)

6. Walk around the _____ . (swim   room   down)

7. Sit on the _____ . (touch   desk   wave)

8. _____ to Janet and touch her. (friend   say   run)

9. _____ that? (who's   point   floor)

10. _____ around the fan. (swim   stop   change)

19

Exercise 2

Reorder the words below to form correct sentences.

1. the television touch **[Sample]** Touch the television.

2. swim desk to the

3. the to point ceiling

4. around run fan the

5. wall a to hop

6. the sit on table

7. the to chalkboard point

8. jump the around class

9. places change the with teacher

10. the hands with shake teacher

Lesson Summary

A	prepositions **around, on**	Swim **around** the desk. Sit **on** the floor.
B	verb be (**is**)	The book **is** on the desk.
C	conjunctive adverb **then**	Run to the fan. **Then** point to the ceiling.
D	question word **who**	**Who's** that?
E	demonstrative pronouns **this** **that**	**This** is Pete **That's** Paula.
F	subjordinate conjunction **if**	**If** I touch the door, hop to the window.
G	**if** clauses	**If I walk to the desk,** jump to me.

H yes/no questions and short answers

Is that Pedro?	

Yes, **it is.**
No, **it's not**

I information questions and answers

Who's	this / that	?

It's Steve.

J contractions

it's	=	it	+	is
that's	=	that	+	is
who's	=	who	+	is

Vocabulary

around	if	student
but	is	swim
ceiling	it's	table
change places	no	that then
class	not	this
desk	on	wall
fan	point	who
floor	room	who's
hop	run	yes
I	sit	

LESSON THREE

You will need

chair   fan   sofa   table   television

Key sentences

Draw a picture to illustrate each Key Sentence.

1. Pretend you're an airplane. **(Sample)**

2. Pretend you're an elephant.

3. Pretend you're a sheep.

4. Pretend you're a monkey.

5. Pretend you're a dog.

6. Pretend you're a cow.

7. Pretend you're a chicken.

8. Pretend you're a cat.

9. Pretend you're a bird.

10. Stand in back of the sofa.

11. Stand in front of the chair.

12. Stand next to the table.

13. Stand on the chair.

14. Now get down.

Participation Exercises

1. Pretend you're an

elephant
airplane

2. Pretend you're a

dog
cat
cow
monkey
bird
sheep
chicken

3. Stand in front of the

television
window
sofa
table
fan

4. Stand in back of the

chair
door
sofa
fan

5. Stand next to the

table
sofa
chair
television
window

6. Stand

in front of
in back of
next to

the chair

Review and Reinforcement

Exercise 1

Copy the sentences below, filling in each with a word.

1. _____ you're a dog. (touch   wave   pretend)

2. Stand in front _____ the chalkboard. (of   to   him)

3. Stand _____ the chair. (on   it   an)

4. Now _____ down. (get   pretend   cow)

5. Pretend _____ a cat. (you   bird   you're)

6. Stand in _____ of the table. (chair   back   change)

7. Stand _____ to the sofa. (front   next   run)

8. Pretend you're _____ airplane. (on   a   an)

9. Stand _____ front of the teacher. (in   an   on)

10. Sit down on the floor next _____ the desk. (to   around   with)

Exercise 2

Reorder the words below to form correct sentences.

1. get now down

2. an you're airplane pretend

3. to point bird the

4. a chicken pretend you're

5. everybody up stand

6. next the to chalkboard stand

7. Fred? of who's front in

8. sofa stand the in of back

9. the of in teacher stand front

10. to jump wall the touch and it

24

Lesson Summary

A	indefinite article **an**	Pretend you're **an** airplane.
B	verb be (**are**)	Pretend you **are** a cat.
C	subject pronoun **you**	Pretend **you** are a dog.
D	prepositions **in back of** **in front of** **next to**	Stand **in back of** the sofa. Stand **in front of** the window. Stand **next to** the table.

E. contractions

you're = you + are

Vocabulary

airplane	cow	next to
an	elephant	pretend
are	get down	sheep
bird	in back of	stand
cat	in front of	you
chicken	monkey	you're

LESSON FOUR

You will need

book   geometric figures (simple set)   key   notebook

Key Sentences

Draw a picture to illustrate each Key Sentence.

1. Touch the triangle and the square. **(Sample)**

2. Pick up the circle.

3. Put the circle down.

4. Point to the rectangle

5. Touch it.

6. Pick it up.

7. Show it to the class.

8. Put it down.

9. Put the circle on the square.

10. Put the triangle next to the rectangle.

11. Give the book to a friend.

12. Show the notebook to a friend.

13. Open the window.

14. Close the window.

15. Pick up the key and open the door.

16. Pass out the triangles.

17. Collect the triangles.

18. Work with your partner.

Participation Exercises

1. Point to the

rectangle
triangle
square
circle

2. Touch the

rectangle
triangle
square
circle

3. Pick up the

circle
rectangle
square
triangle

    Put the **circle** down.

4. Pick up the

square
rectangle
triangle
circle

    Put it down.

5. Give the

rectangle
triangle
circle
square

    to your friend.

6. Show the

circle
triangle
square
rectangle

    to your friend.

7. Point to the

| circle |
| square |
| triangle |
| rectangle |

Touch it.
Pick it up.
Show it to the class.
Put it down.

8. Put the circle

| on |
| next to |

the

| square |
| triangle |
| rectangle |

9. Open the

| door |
| window |
| book |
| notebook |

Close the **door.**

Review and Reinforcement

Exercise 1

Copy the phrases below, completing each one with a phrase from the list.

1. Pick _____
2. Point _____
3. Open the _____
4. Give me _____
5. Touch the _____
6. Put the triangle _____
7. Put _____
8. Pass _____
9. Pick it _____
10. Give the _____

LIST
up
window
to the triangle
circle
down
out of squares
the rectangle
it down
key to your friend
up the circle

28

Exercise 2

Reorder the words below to form correct sentences.

1. it pick up

2. open door the

3. the close window

4. a on friend sit

5. triangle up the pick

6. down the put square

7. class to it the show

8. pretend elephant you're an

9. in of a friend back stand

10. give to book teacher the the

Lesson Summary

A	possessive adjective **your**	Show me **your** triangle.
B	geometric figures **circle** **rectangle** **square** **triangle**	Put the **circle** on the **rectangle** Put the **triangle** next to the **square**
C	two-word verbs **pick up** **put down** **pass out**	**Pick up** the circle. **Pick** it **up**. **Put down** the square. **Put** it **down**. **Pass out** the triangles.

D sentence pattern: to + indirect object

verb	direct object	indirect object
Give Show	the book	**to a friend**

Vocabulary

book	key	pick up	square
circle	notebook	put	triangle
close	open	put down	work
collect	partner	rectangle	your
give	pass out	show	

LESSON FIVE

You will need

chair   geometric figures (simple set)   television

Key Sentences

Draw a picture to illustrate each Key Sentence.

1. Pull your hair. **(Sample)**

2. Touch an ear.

3. Touch your ears.

4. Stand in front of me and pull my nose.

5. Stand in back of a friend and pull her hair.

6. Stand in front of a friend and touch his nose.

7. Pull a friend's hair

8. Go to the window.

9. Come with me to the door.

10. Put the triangle on the rectangle.

11. Now put the triangle under the rectangle.

12. Put the circle between the square and the rectangle.

13. Distribute the squares.

14. Pick up the squares.

Participation Exercises

1. Pull your

hair
nose
ear
ears

2. Pull

my
your

hair
nose
ear
ears

3. Stand in front of a friend and pull his

nose
hair
ear
ears

4. Stand in back of a friend and pull her

nose
hair
ear
ears

5. Pull your friend's

nose
hair
ear
ears

6. Go to the

door
window
television
chair

7. Put the circle between the

triangle
rectangle
square

and the

square
triangle
rectangle

8. Put the circle | on
under
next to | the | square
triangle
rectangle |

9. How do you say _____ in | English ?
Spanish
_____* |

*Students write their native language in this blank.

Visual Practice Exercise

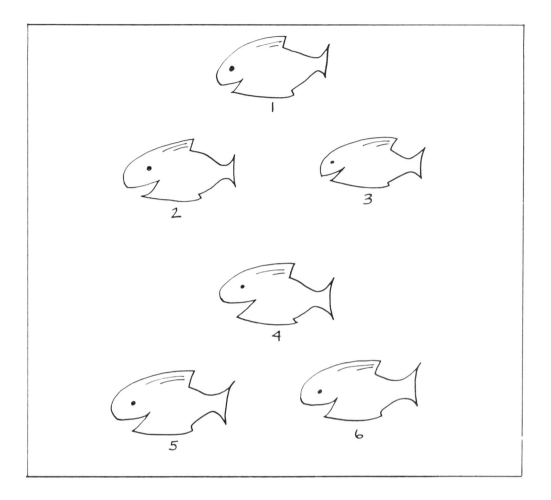

Note - Demonstrate for your students that the first fish should be colored **red** and gesture for your students to color their first fish red. The second fish is colored **green,** etc.

1. red	2. green	3. white
4. black	5. yellow	6. blue

Listen and Perform

A	Touch Point to	the **red** fish.	
B	Put the coin	on in front of in back of under	the **blue** fish.
C	Put the coin between the **red** fish and the **green** fish.		

34

Visual Practice Exercises

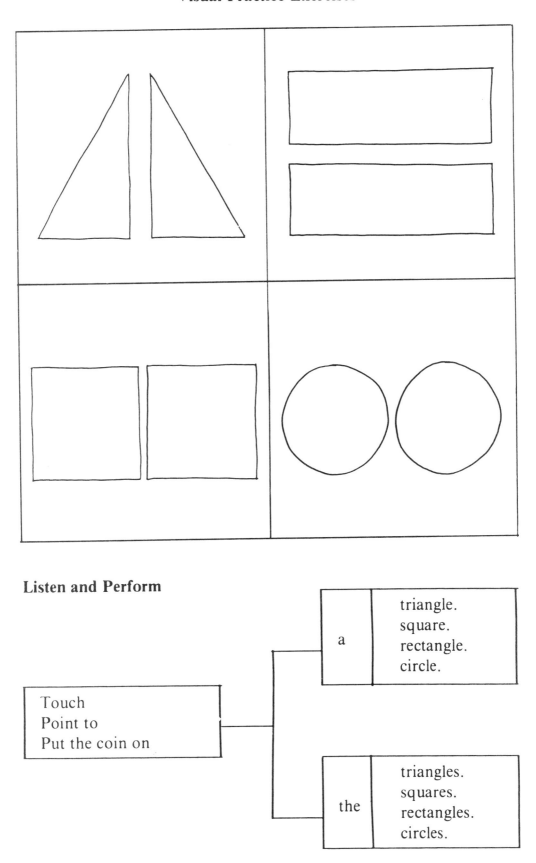

Listen and Perform

Touch Point to Put the coin on		a	triangle. square. rectangle. circle.
		the	triangles. squares. rectangles. circles.

Review and Reinforcement

Exercise 1

Copy the phrases below, completing each one with a phrase from the list.

1. Stand in front of me _____

2. How do you _____

3. Come with _____

4. Put the coin on _____

5. Put the triangle _____

6. Pull a _____

7. Touch your _____

8. Put the circle between the square _____

9. Stand in back of Sandra and _____

10. Point _____

LIST

the red fish.

say "cat" in Spanish?

ears.

to an ear.

pull her nose.

and the triangle.

me to the chalkboard.

and pull my nose.

under the circle.

friend's hair.

Exercise 2

Reorder the words below to form correct sentences.

1. touch ears your

2. me places with change

3. hair pull friend's a

4. point friend's to nose a

5. triangle rectangle the the under put

6. put circle the on the square

7. and the the square touch triangle

8. desk cry the next stand and to

9. key up door the pick the open and

10. me my and front in of stand pull nose

Lesson Summary

A	prepositions **between, under**	Put the circle **between** the triangle and the square. Put the circle **under** the triangle.
B	colors **black green yellow blue white red**	Touch the **red** fish. Point to the **green** fish.
C	parts of the body **nose ear hair**	Pull your **hair.** Point to an **ear.** Touch my **nose.**
D	possessive form of nouns **'s**	Pull a **friend's** hair.
E	**a/the**	Touch **a** triangle. Touch **the** triangles.
F	question word **how**	**How** do you say "book " in Spanish?
G	impersonal pronoun **you**	How do **you** say "cat" in Spanish?
H	auxiliary **do**	How **do** you say "dog" in Spanish?

I   possessive adjectives (partial list)

Walk to	Pedri Maria me	and pull	**his** **her** **my**	nose

37

Vocabulary

between	do	hair	pull
black	ear	her	red
blue	English	his	Spanish
coin	fish	how	under
come	go	my	white
distribute	green	nose	yellow

LESSON SIX

You will need

book	chalk	eraser	flower
geometric figures (simple set)			notebook
paper		pen	pencil

Key Sentences

Draw a picture to illustrate each Key Sentence.

1. Point to a friend. **(Sample)**

2. Give your friend the flower.

3. Now show your friend a book.

4. Take a pen from a friend's desk and put it on your desk.

5. Pick up the pen.

6. Write your name in the notebook.

7. Take out a sheet of paper.

8. Draw a triangle between a happy face and a sad face.

9. Draw a boy next to a girl.

10. Draw a man next to a woman.

11. Draw a triangle in a circle.

12. Draw a triangle and a circle.

13. Pick up the pencil and draw a circle under a rectangle.

14. Pick up the eraser and erase the circle.

15. Show a piece of chalk to the class.

16. Tell me your mother's name.

Participation Exercises

1. Draw a

happy face
sad face
television set
flower
cat

2. Pick up the pencil and draw a

circle
triangle
fish
square

   Now erase it.

3. Draw a

flower
fish

   in a

square
triangle
rectangle

4. Give a friend the

book
notebook
pen
pencil
eraser

5. Show a friend the

pen
pencil
book
notebook
eraser

6. Tell me your

mother's
father's
brother's
sister's

   name

Visual Practice Exercises

John   Helen

Mark   Carla   Donna

Listen and Repeat

A	1. John is Carla's father. 2. Helen is Carla's mother. 3. Mark is Carla's brother. 4. Donna is Carla's sister. 5. John is a man. 6. Helen is a woman. 7. Mark is a boy. 8. Carla is a girl, and Donna is too.

Listen and Perform

B	Touch Put the coin on Tell me the name of Whisper the name of Point to	Carla's	mother. father. brother. sister.

Ask and Answer

C	Who's Carla's **mother**?	➡	**Helen** is.

Visual Practice Exercises

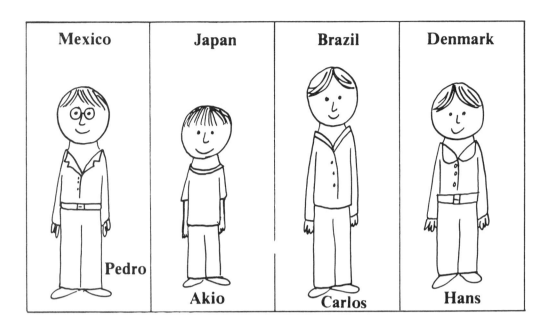

Listen and Perform

A	Touch Point to Tell me the name of Put the coin on	the boy who's from **Brazil.**

Ask and Answer

B	Who's from **Mexico**?	➡	**Pedro** is.
C	Is **Pedro** from **Mexico**?	➡	Yes, he is. No, he isn't.

Review and Reinforcement

Exercise 1

Copy the sentences below, filling in the blanks with words from the list.

1. Take _____ a sheet of paper.

2. My _____ is a boy.

3. Draw a _____ face.

4. Take a book _____ a friend's desk.

5. Draw a man next to a _____

6. Your _____ is a girl.

7. Write your _____ name.

8. Give me a sheet _____ paper.

9. _____ a flower in front of a fish.

10. Show me a piece of _____ .

LIST
brother
from
of
draw
woman
sister
Brazil
happy
in
say
tell
out
too
chalk
mother's

Exercise 2
Reorder the words below to form correct sentences.

1. name your tell mother's me

2. flower my sister give the

3. father circle show now your the

4. out sheet paper take of a

5. in your notebook write the name

6. the who's Mexico touch man from

7. square a face a in happy draw

8. up pick pencil draw circle a the and

9. me in my touch and front stand nose of

10. Ted's me desk triangle take a give to from it and

43

Lesson Summary

A	family relations	**mother father brother sister**	Put the circle on Carla's **father.**
B	countries	**Brazil Denmark Mexico Japan**	Tell me the name of the boy who's from **Brazil.**
C	relative pronoun	**who**	Touch the student **who's** from Japan.
D	**who** clauses		Point to the student **who's from Mexico.**
E	adverb	**too**	Frank is a boy, and Richard is **too.**
F	two-word verb	**take out**	**Take out** a sheet of paper.

G indirect object sentence patterns

verb	direct object	indirect object
Give Show	the flower	**to your friend.**

verb	indirect object	direct object
Give Show	**your friend**	the flower.

H information questions and short answers

Who's Pete's mother?		Carla **is.**

I yes/no questions and short answers

Is Pedro from Mexico?	➡	Yes, **he is.**
		No, **he isn't**

J contraction

isn't = is + not

44

Vocabulary

boy	father	Mexico	sheet
Brazil	flower	mother	sister
brother	from	name	take
chalk	girl	of	take out
Denmark	happy	paper	tell
draw	in	pen	too
erase	isn't	pencil	who's
eraser	Japan	piece	woman
face	man	sad	write

LESSON SEVEN

You will need

chair   eraser   paper   pencil   table   television

Key Sentences

Draw a picture to illustrate each Key Sentence.

1. Sing a song by the Beatles. **(Sample)**

2. Whistle "Happy Birthday."

3. Hum "My Bonnie Lies over the Ocean."

4. Pull your hair and cry.

5. Point to your nose and laugh.

6. Stand in front of us and pull our hair.

7. Draw a small heart between two big circles.

8. Jump to the window, touching your nose.

9. Walk around the room, pointing to the ceiling.

10. Touch something on the table.

11. Point to someone and say "hello."

Participation Exercises

1. Pull your

| hair |
| nose |
| ear |
| ears |

and cry

2. Pretend you're a

| dog |
| cat |
| cow |
| chicken |

and laugh.

3. Sing a song by   *

_____
_____
_____
_____

**

4.

| Sing |
| Hum |
| Whistle |

_____
_____
_____
_____

5. Stand

| in front of |
| in back of |
| next to |

us and pull our

| hair |
| noses |
| ears |

  *   Students write in the names of singers from their own country.
**   Students write in songs from their own country.

6. Draw a

| big |
| small |

| key |
| fish |
| happy face |
| sad face |
| flower |

7.

| Hop
Jump
Walk
Run | to the | door,
window,
t.v.,
chair, | touching your nose
pointing to an ear
laughing
crying
waving to a friend
singing a song by _____* |

* Students fill in the blank with a singer from their own country.

Visual Practice Exercise

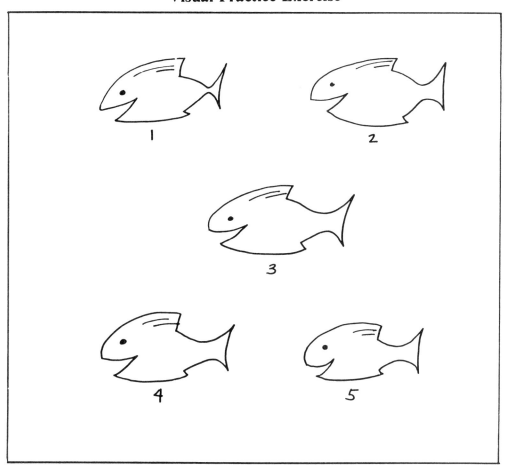

1. brown	2. orange	3. pink
4. gray	5. purple	

Listen and Perform

A	Point to _____ Touch	the **pink** fish

B	Put the coin	on in front of in back of under	the **gray** fish.

C	Put the coin between the **brown** fish and the **orange** fish.

Visual Practice Exercises

Listen and Perform

A	Touch the student who's wearing	a	skirt dress blouse shirt T-shirt
			pants jeans

B	Touch someone who's wearing something	red green white yellow blue brown orange

Visual Practice Exercises

| | Tony | Henry | Robin | Norman |
| Maurice | Leonard | Richard | Gerald |

Listen and Perform

A	Touch Point to Tell me the name of Whisper the name of	the man who has the	big	**heart.**
			small	

Ask and Answer

B	Who has the	big	**rectangle?**	**Tony** does.
		small		
C	Does **Tony** have the	big	**heart?**	Yes, he does.
		small		No, he doesn't.

51

Review and Reinforcement

Copy the sentences below, completing each one with a phrase from the list.

1. Walk around the room, touching _____ .

2. Point to your _____ .

3. Him a _____ .

4. Stand in front of _____ .

5. Draw a small flower _____ .

6. Touch something on _____ .

7. Point _____ .

8. Jump to the door, _____ .

9. Whistle _____ .

10. Tell me the name of the boy _____ .

List

song by the Beatles.
under a big triangle.
a song.
your ear.
from Japan.
to someone.
nose and laugh.
us and pull our hair.
the floor.
pulling your hair.

Exercise 2
Reorder the words below to form correct sentences.

1. singing the around hop table

2. your give flower the sister

3. something the on touch desk

4. now to it the class show

5. song sing Beatles the by a

6. ears a then and friend's pull cry

7. room, around touching jump nose the your

8. stand our hair pull us front in of and

9. to close walk it window and the

10. chair back point the the to ceiling of in stand and

Lesson Summary

A	clothing **blouse pants skirt dress shirt jeans t-shirt**	Point to someone who's wearing a blue **shirt**.
B	colors **brown orange pink gray purple**	Touch the **pink** fish.
C	adjectives **big small**	Draw a **small** heart under a **big** triangle.
D	preposition **by**	Sing a song **by** the Beatles.
E	verb form **has**	Touch the student who **has** the big square.
F	possessive adjective **our**	Stand in back of me and Ted and pull **our** hair.
G	object pronoun **us**	Stand in front of me and Sue and say "hello" to **us**.
H	indefinite pronouns **someone something**	Touch **someone** who's wearing **something** yellow.
I	**who** clauses	Tell me the name of the student **who** has the small triangle.
J	present continuous (**who's wearing**)	Touch the student **who's wearing** a red skirt.
K	adjective phrases with **ing**	Jump to the window, **touching your nose.**
L	auxiliary **does**	**Does** Tony have the small heart?

M yes/no questions and short answers

| Does Tony have the big triangle? | ➡ | Yes, **he does.** |
| | | No, **he doesn't.** |

N information questions and short answers

| **Who has** the big triangle? | ➡ | Paula **does.** |

O   formation of **ing** form

base form	ing form
jump touch stand wear point show	**jumping** **touching** **standing** **wearing** **pointing** **showing**
sit hop run swim	**sitting** **hopping** **running** **swimming**
sit hop run swim	**sitting** **hopping** **running** **swimming**
shake come wave give	**shaking** **coming** **waving** **giving**

P   contraction   **doesn't** = does + not

Vocabulary

big	gray	pants	something
blouse	has	pink	song
brown	heart	purple	T-shirt
by	hum	shirt	t.v.
cry	jeans	sing	us
does	laugh	skirt	wear
doesn't	orange	small	whistle
dress	our	someone	

LESSON EIGHT

You will need

chair   geometric figures (double set)   sofa   table   television

Key Sentences

Draw a picture to illustrate each Key Sentence.

1. Breathe in, breathe out, relax. **(Sample)**

2. Jump to the window and stretch.

3. Hop to the door and clap.

4. Stoop in back of the chair.

5. Close your eyes.

6. Open your mouth.

7. Point to a foot.

8. Touch both feet.

9. Pull only one ear.

10. Now pull both ears.

11. Put your hands on your ears.

12. Tell someone to jump and point to the person who's jumping.

Participation Exercises

1. Jump to the

door
window
television
table
sofa

and clap.

2. Stand

in front of
in back of
next to

the chair and stretch.

3. Stoop

in front of
in back of
next to

the chair.

4. Run to the

table
sofa
television
window
door

and breathe in.

Now breathe out.

5.

Cry
Hum
Laugh
Sing
Whistle
Breathe in
Breathe out
Clap
Stretch
Wave
Stoop

6. Point to

an ear
your ears
an eye
your eyes
a hand
your hands
a foot
your feet

7. Touch

an ear
both ears
an eye
both eyes
a foot
both feet

8. Touch the

triangles
squares
circles
rectangles

Pick up only one, not both.
Now put it down.

9.

Open
Close

your

mouth
hands
eyes

10. Walk around the room,

crying
singing
humming
whistling
clapping

Visual Practice Exercises

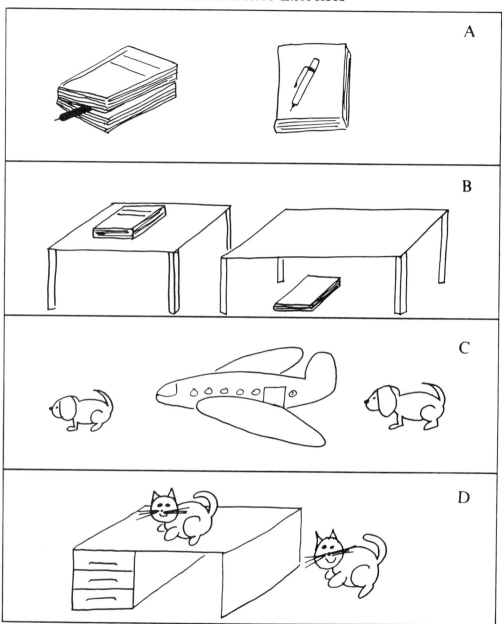

Listen and Perform

A	Touch the pen that's	on	the book.
		in	
B	Point to the book that's	on	the desk.
		under	
C	Touch the dog that's	in front of	the airplane.
		in back of	
D	Point to the cat that's	on	the desk.
		next to	

Review and Reinforcement

Exercise 1

Copy the phrases below, filling in each blank with a word.

1. Close your _____ . (purple   has   eyes)

2. Draw a happy face with _____ one ear.
   (pink   only   small)

3. Touch _____ feet. (heart   does   both)

4. Open your _____ . (laugh   our   mouth)

5. _____ next to the desk. (skirt   wear   stoop)

6. Stand in back of the sofa and _____ in.
   (whistle   breathe   hum)

7. Show a _____ to the class. (foot   feet   pants)

8. _____ someone to jump to the door. (clap   tell   relax)

9. Touch the _____ who's sitting in front of you.
   (gray   person   shirt)

10. Stand in front of me and _____
    (stretch   piece   erase)

Exercise 2

Reorder the words below to form correct sentences

1. your mouth close

2. both to eyes point

3. next stoop the sofa to

4. one ear, both pull only not

5. feet on your the put desk

6. hands your your ears put on

7. Spanish? say do in "dog" how you

8. sad a eyes draw big with face

9. the triangle person you next who's the to give sitting to

10. someone crying person who's cry point tell and the to to

Lesson Summary

A	countries	**Columbia France England Spain**	Tell me the names of the boys who are from **Spain.**
B	parts of the body	**eye hand foot mouth feet**	Point to an **eye.**
C	present continuous **(who's - ing)**		Point to the person **who's jumping.**
D	relative pronoun **that**		Touch the book **that's** on the table.
E	clauses	**that** **who**	Point to the book **that's on the floor.** Point to the boys **who are from France.**

F   yes / no questions and short answers

Are Pedro and Carlos from Spain?

Yes. **they are.**
No. **they aren't.**

G   information questions and short answers

Who's from Spain?

Pedro and Carlos **are.**

H   contraction

aren't = are + not

I   irregular plural

singular	plural
foot	**feet**

Vocabulary

aren't	England	mouth	stoop
both	eye	one	stretch
breathe in	feet	only	tell
breathe out	foot	person	that
clap	France	relax	that's
Colombia	hand	Spain	

LESSON NINE

You will need

| bracelet | cap | geometric figures (double set) | | hat |
| necklace | paper | pencil | tie | watch |

Key Sentences

Draw a picture to illustrate each Key Sentence.

1. Draw a small heart under a big hat. **(Sample)**

2. Put on the tie.

3. Take it off.

4. Put on the cap, the necklace, the bracelet and the watch.

5. Take them off.

6. Pick up the square and the circle.

7. Put them down.

8. Pick up the triangle but don't show it to the class.

9. Now show it to the class.

10. Pick up the circle and the rectangle.

11. Put down only the circle.

12. Now put down the rectangle.

13. Tell two people to cry and point to the people who are crying.

14. Put your hand on your shoulder.

15. Draw a happy face with one tooth next to a sad face with three teeth.

16. Draw a girl with a heart on her forehead, a triangel on her chin, and a flower on each cheek.

Participation Exercises

1.   Put on the

necklace
hat
cap
bracelet
tie
watch

Take it off

2.   Put on the

hat
tie
cap
bracelet

and the

necklace
cap
watch
hat

Take off only the **hat.**
Now take off the **necklace.**

63

3.　Point to the

triangles
rectangles
squares
circles

Touch them.
Pick them up.
Show them to the class.
Put them down.

4.　Pick up the

triangle
square
circle
rectangle

and the

circle
triangle
rectangle
square

Put down only the **triangle.**
Now put down the **circle.**

5.　Pick up the

triangle
rectangle
circle
square

but don't show it to the class.

Now show it to the class.

6.　Touch

your forehead
your chin
a shoulder
a cheek
a tooth
two teeth

Visual Practice Exercises

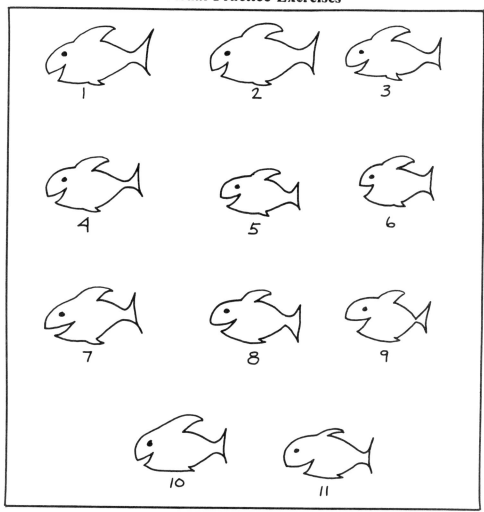

1. red	2. green	3. white	4. black	5. yellow	6. blue
7. brown	8. gray	9. orange	10. pink	11. purple	

Listen and Perform

A	Touch Point to	the **red fish.**

B	Put the coin	on in front of in back of under	the **blue** fish.

C	Put the coin between the **red** fish and the **green** fish.

65

Review and Reinforcement

Exercise 1

Copy the phrases below, filling in the blanks with words from the list.

1. Put on the _____ .

2. Take _____

3. Don't _____

4. Put _____

5. Draw a girl with a star _____

6. Take it _____

7. Point _____

8. Draw a happy face with a heart on _____

9. Put on _____

10. Tell me the name of the person _____ .

LIST

who's wearing
a cap
hat
on her chin
them off
the bracelet
on the tie
touch your
shoulders
off
each cheek
to your
forehead

Exercise 2

Reorder the words below to form correct sentences

1. take off it

2. on tie put the

3. down the only rectangle put

4. touch England from boy the who's

5. door nose your the with touch

6. who's jeans point the wearing to boy

7. up both and square triangle the the pick

8. face one draw a eye sad only with

9. tell them point people to two hop and to

10. me but don't up the show to it circle pick

Lesson Summary

A	clothing	**bracelet necklace** **cap** **tie** **hat** **watch**	Put on the **hat**
B	colors	**red** **black** **brown** **green yellow orange** **white blue** **purple** **gray** **pink**	Put the circle on the **pink** fish.
C	parts of the body	**shoulder tooth teeth** **forehead chin cheek**	Draw a happy face with a star on its **forehead.**
D	conjunction **but**		Pick up the circle **but** don't show it to the class.
E	object pronoun **them**		Pick up the squares and show **them** to the class.
F	present continuous **(who are -ing)**		Point to the people **who are crying.**
G	two-word verbs	**put on** **take off**	**Put on** the hat. **Put** it **on.** **Take off** the tie. **Take** it **off.**
H	indefinite determiner **each**		Draw a girl with a heart on **each** cheek.

I. irregular plurals

singular	plural
person tooth	people teeth

Vocabulary

bracelet	forehead	take off
cap	hat	teeth
cheek	necklace	them
chin	people	tooth
don't	put on	tie
each	shoulder	watch

LESSON TEN

You will need

paper   pencil

Key Sentences

Draw a picture to illustrate each Key Sentence.

1 1. Sneeze two times. **(Sample)**

2. Cough four times

3. Count the buttons on your shirt.

4. Unbutton your shirt.

5. Button your shirt.

6. Point to two friends.

7. Stand in front of them and pull their hair.

8. Add the numbers seven and three.

9. Draw a triangle around the sum.

10. Write the number that comes after five.

11. Write the number that comes before six.

12. Write the number that comes between eight and ten.

13. Draw a clock on a wall.

14. Draw two happy faces, one with big eyes and one without any eyes.

15. Draw a hat on the face that doesn't have any eyes.

Participation Exercises

1.

Jump	2
hop	3
clap	4
sneeze	5
cough	6

times

2. Draw

| 2 |
| 3 |
| 4 |
| 5 |
| 6 |

| hearts |
| triangles |
| eyes |
| hats |
| fans |

3. Add

| 1 |
| 2 |
| 8 |
| 4 |
| 5 |

and

| 5 |
| 7 |
| 3 |
| 6 |
| 10 |

Draw a

| circle |
| triangle |
| rectangle |
| square |

around the sum.

4. Write the number that comes **before**

| 5 |
| 8 |
| 2 |
| 7 |
| 10 |

5. Write the number that comes **after**

| 6 |
| 1 |
| 3 |
| 9 |
| 4 |

6. Write the number that comes

| **before** |
| **after** |

| 1 |
| 2 |
| 3 |
| 4 |
| 5 |

| 6 |
| 7 |
| 8 |
| 9 |
| 10 |

70

Visual Practice Exercises

Listen and Perform

A	Touch Put the coin on 7 o'clock. Point to

Ask and Answer

B	What time is it?

➡ It's 7 o'clock.

Visual Practice Exercises

1. birds	2. happy faces	3. tables	4. fans	5. doors
6. eyes	7. ties	8. airplanes	9. hearts	10. televisions
11. sad faces	12. pens	13. windows	14. cats	15. pencils
16. girls	17. circles	18. buttons	19. caps	20. squares
21. hats	22. chairs	23. flowers	24. triangles	25. rectangles

Listen and Perform

A	Count the **birds** and write the number in your notebook.
B	Draw **two birds**.

72

Visual Practice Exercises

Listen and Perform

			two three four five	dogs
A	Touch Point to Put the coin on Tell me the names of Whisper the names of	the girls who have		cats.

		two three four five			Yes, They do.
B	Do **Karen** and **Rose** have		dogs cats	?	No, they don't.

73

Visual Practice Exercises

Spain

Maria   Carmen

France

Pauline   Claudette

England

Margaret   Barbara

Columbia

Gloria   Virginia

Listen and Perform

A	Touch Point to Tell me the names of Whisper the names of Put the coin on	the girls who are from **Spain.**

Ask and Answer

B	Who's from **Spain?**	➡	**Maria** and **Carmen** are.

C	Are **Maria** and **Carmen** from **Spain?**	➡	Yes, they are.
			No, they aren't.

Review and Reinforcement

Exercise 1

Copy the phrases below, filling in the blanks with words from the list.

1. Stand in front of two friends and pull _____ hair.

2. _____ the numbers seven and nine.

3. Draw a square around the _____ of the numbers.

4. Draw a happy face _____ any eyes.

5. Cough two _____ .

6. Button your _____

7. Seven comes _____ six.

8. Write the number that comes _____ three and five.

9. _____ the buttons on your shirt.

10. Draw a clock on a _____ .

LIST

sum	only	between
wall	add	sister
their	small	shirt
count	something	times
them	after	without

Exercise 2

Reorder the words below to form correct sentences

1. times three cough

2. add six numbers the and two

3. students class the the count in

4. girl a big nose a draw with

5. between desk teacher the and stand the

6. next sum daw square the to a

7. write ten comes number after that the

8. clock that's table the touch the on

9. hands a red with who's shake wearing something person

10. stand pull hair them their front in of and

Lesson Summary

A	prepositions	**after** **before** **without**	Write the number that comes **before/after** eight. Draw a happy face **without** eyes.
B	indefinite determiner **any**		Draw a sad face without **any** ears.
C	negative prefix **un**		**Un**button your shirt.
D	verb form **have**		Tell me the names of the boys who **have** two cats.
E	present tense (3rd per sing.)		Write the number that **comes** after six.
F	telling time (on the hour)		**It's five o'clock.**
G	impersonal pronoun **it** (in time expressions)		**It's** seven o'clock.
H	question word **what + time**		**What time** is it?
I	clauses	**that** **who**	Write the number **that** comes after five. Touch the boys **who** have two cats.

J   numbers 1 — 12

1	one	7	seven
2	two	8	eight
3	three	9	nine
4	four	10	ten
5	five	11	eleven
6	six	12	twelve

K   yes/no questions and short answers

Do Alice and Laura have two dogs?

Yes, **they do.**
No, **they don't.**

Vocabulary

add	cough	number	three
after	count	o'clock	times
any	eight	seven	twelve
before	eleven	six	two
button (n)	five	sneeze	unbutton
button (v)	four	sum	what time
clock	have	ten	without
comes	nine	their	

77

LESSON ELEVEN

You will need

chair   desk   fan   sofa   table

Role Reversal — 1

(In **role reversal,** individual students get an opportunity to give commands to the instructor and other students. **As a hint,** invite students **who are ready** to come up to the front of the class and utter one-word English commands in the first set to direct the movements of other students or the instructor. As a prompt, they may wish to read the English commands as they are printed.)

1.
Stand Up
Walk
Stop
Turn around
Run
Stop
Jump
Swim
Hop
Sit down

2.
Sing
Hum
Whistle
Laugh
Cry
Breathe in
Breathe out
Stoop
Clap
Wave
Stretch
Cough
Sneeze

3.   Walk to the
door
window
chalkboard
sofa
teacher

4. Jump to the

television
chair
table
fan
window

5. Swim to the

door
window
chair
television
sofa

6.

Walk
Jump
Swim

to the

door
window
desk
fan
chalkboard
sofa
table
teacher

7.

Walk
Jump
Swim

to

a friend
me

and

say "hello"
shake hands
wave
stretch
cry

8. Pretend you're a/an

elephant
airplane
dog
cat
cow
bird
chicken
sheep

LESSON TWELVE

chair   desk   fan   paper   pencil   sofa   table   television

Role Reversal — 2

1. Run to the

door
window
desk
chalkboard
chair
sofa
television

2. Hop to the

chair
table
door
window
fan

3.

Walk	to me and	shake hands
Jump		say "hello"
Run		whisper "hello"
Hop		touch me
Swim		point to me

4.   Point to the

door
window
desk
chair
teacher
chalkboard
fan
floor
ceiling
sofa
television

5.   Touch the

door
window
desk
chair
teacher
fan
floor
chair
sofa

6.   Draw a

happy face
sad face
television
flower
cat
key
fish
circle
square
rectangle
triangle

LESSON THIRTEEN

You will need

chair   desk   fan   sofa   table   television

Role Reversal — 3

1.

Walk Jump Hop Swim Run	around the	room table chair desk teacher

2.

Walk Jump Hop Swim Run	to around	a friend me

3. Stand **in front of** the

chair desk table door window fan television sofa

4. Stand **in back of** the

teacher
desk
table
sofa
chair
fan

5. Stand next to the

door
window
chair
table
desk
teacher
sofa

6. Stand

in front of
in back of
next to

a friend
me

and

breathe in
laugh
sneeze
cough
cry
sing
clap

7.

Walk
Jump
Hop
Swim

around me,

crying
singing
humming
clapping
whistling

LESSON FOURTEEN

You will need

book   bracelet   cap   chair   eraser   flower
geometric figures (simple set)   hat   necklace   notebook
pen   pencil   sofa   television   tie   watch

Role Reversal — 4

1. | Touch
   | Point to | your | nose
   mouth
   eye
   eyes
   ear
   ears
   forehead
   chin
   cheek
   shoulder
   teeth
   foot
   feet |

2. Put on the | hat
   tie
   bracelet
   cap
   watch
   necklace |

   Take it off.

3. | Point to
   | Touch | the | circle
   square
   triangle
   rectangle |

4. Point to the

circle
square
triangle
rectangle

Pick it up.
Show it to the class.
Put it down

5. Put the **circle**

on
under
next to

the **square**

6. Put the **circle** between the **square** and the **triangle**.

7.

Give
Show

me the

circle
square
rectangle
triangle
pen
pencil
book
notebook
flower
eraser

8.

Hop
Jump
Walk
Run
Swim

to the

door
window
television
chair
sofa
chalkboard
teacher

and then

touch your nose
pull your hair
pretend you're a dog
point to the ceiling
sit on the floor
wave to me

LESSON FIFTEEN

You will need

beard   book   can   crown   earring   glasses   ring   wig

Key Sentences

Draw a picture to illustrate each Key Sentence.

1. Shake the can. **(Sample)**

2. Touch your neck.

3. Point to your head.

4. Put on the crown and pretend you're a king.

5. Take it off.

6. Put on the wig.

7. Point to a friend.

8. Give your friend the ring.

9. Put on the glasses.

10. Take them off.

11. Draw a sad face with a beard, an earring, and a mustache.

12. Draw a flower.

13. Draw another flower.

14. Draw a circle.

15. Draw some circles.

16. Draw a fish with a chair on its head.

17. Draw a girl with only one leg. She has a big foot with only three toes.

18. Touch one of your arms with a finger and a thumb.

19. Point to your belly and touch your back.

20. Hold a book against your chest.

Participation Exercises

1.   Put on the

| wig |
| earring |
| glasses |
| beard |
| crown |
| ring |

and

| sing |
| laugh |
| cry |
| stoop |
| hum |

Take

| it / them |

off.

87

2. Point to your

head
nose
mouth
neck

3. Shake

the can
your head
a hand
your hands
your feet

4. Draw a

circle
heart
flower
chair

Now draw another **circle.**

5. Draw a

sad face
happy face

with

a beard
a mustache
an earring
earrings
glasses

6. Draw a girl wearing

a hat
a necklace
a crown
glasses
earrings

7. Touch

an arm
a leg
two fingers
your thumb
your back
your belly

Visual Practice Exercises

Drawing Activity: Close your book. Your partner will choose a **picture** from this page and will tell you what to draw. For example, your partner may say to you, "Draw a circle." Or, your partner may say, "Draw some circles."

Draw	a **circle.**
	some **circles.**

Visual Practice Exercises

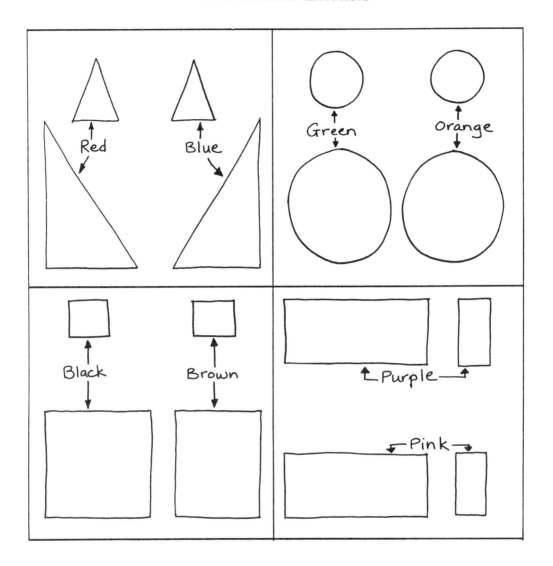

red	blue	green	orange
black	brown	purple	pink

Listen and Perform

Touch Put the coin on the Point to	big ——————— **red** triangle. small

Review and Reinforcement

Exercise 1

Copy the sentences below filling each blank with a word.

1. Shake the _____ . (sum   back   can)

2. Draw a happy face _____ a crown. (sneezing   wearing   counting)

3. Put on the _____ . (neck   wig   button)

4. Draw _____ circle. (two   small   another)

5. Put on the glasses and take _____ off. (her   him   them)

6. _____ the book against your chest. (stoop   their   hold)

7. Shake your _____ . (before   head   after)

8. Draw a hand with four _____ . (fingers   legs   toes)

9. Draw _____ big triangles. (this   some   a)

10. Draw a girl wearing only one _____ . (both   person   earring.)

Exercise 2

Reorder the words below to form correct sentences.

1. take off them

2. wig on put the

3. another me pencil give

4. small draw some flowers

5. the shake five can times

6. head your hand touch one with

7. draw with beard a a happy face

8. before that number seven write the comes

9. head draw fish heart its a on a with

10. desk sitting person the to the next who's touch

Lesson Summary

A	a/some	Draw **a** flower/Draw **some** flowers.
B	adjective phrases	Draw a happy face **with a beard.**
C	possessive adjectives **its**	Draw a fish with a chair on **its** head.
D	preposition **against**	Hole the book **against** your chest.
E	parts of the body **arm leg finger toe back belly chest**	Point to the ceilng with two **fingers.**
F	indefinite determiners **another some**	Draw a circle. Now draw **another circle.** Draw **some** hearts.

G sentence pattern

Put the coin on the	**big**	**red**	triangle

Vocabulary

against	belly	finger	king	shake
another	can	glasses	leg	thumb
arm	chest	head	mustache	toe
back	crown	hold	neck	wig
beard	earring	its	ring	

LESSON SIXTEEN

You will need

bag   bracelet   box   can   candle   cigarettes
earring   flower   geometric figures (double set)   matches
paper   pen   pencil   purse   ring   watch

Key Sentences

Draw a picture to illustrate each Key Sentence.

1. Pick up the matches. **(Sample)**

2. Take out a match.

3. Light the candle.

4. Blow it out.

5. Put a cigarette in your pocket.

6. Take it out.

7. Put your watch in the bag.

8. Take it out.

9. Put the can in the purse.

10. Take it out.

11. Put your pen in the box and shake it.

12. Pick up two triangles.

13. Put one triangle on the floor and put the other on your head.

14. Touch the triangle that's on your head and point to the triangle that's on the floor.

15. Draw a clock showing five to seven.

16. Draw another clock, showing ten after eight.

17. Draw a happy face smoking a cigarette.

Participation Exercises

1. Light

a match
the candle

Blow it out.

2. Put the

candle
cigarettes
matches
pen
ring

in the bag.

3. Take the

candle
cigarettes
matches
pen
ring

out of the bag

4. Put the

candle
cigarettes
matches
ring
earring

in your pocket

   Take

it/them

out

5. Put the

can
candle
flower
bracelet
watch

in the

purse
box
bag

   Take it out.

6. Pick up both

triangles
circles
squares
rectangles

Put one **triangle** on the floor and put the other on the table.
Touch the **triangle** that's on the table and point to the **triangle** that's on the floor.

94

Visual Practice Exercises

1. chair	2. triangle	3. watch	4. cat	5. hat
6. door	7. flower	8. fish	9. television	10. airplane
11. cap	12 sheep	13. clock	14. match	15. elephant
16. bag	17. heart	18. fan	19. button	20. cow

Ask and Answer

A		What's	this	?		It's a **hat.**
			that			
B		Is this a **clock?**				Yes, it is.
						No, it isn't.

95

Visual Practice Exercises

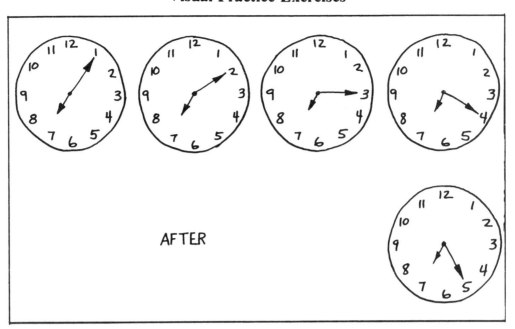

AFTER

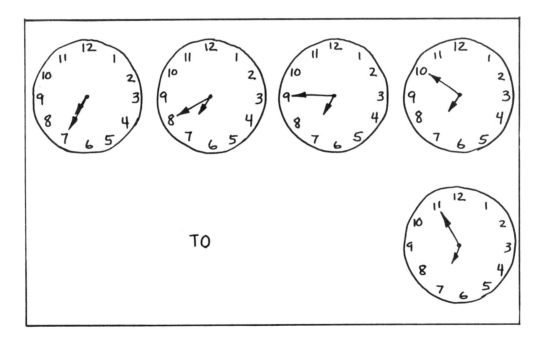

TO

Listen and Perform

A	Touch Put the coin on Point to	five	after	seven
			to	

Ask and Answer

B	What time is it?	➡	It's **five** after **seven**

96

Ask and Answer

A	Where's Sam?	➡	He's next to the table.
B	Where's Rose?	➡	She's in front of the table.
C	Where's the cat?	➡	It's on the table.
D	Where are Anita and Janet?	➡	They're in back of the table.

Review and Reinforcement

Exercise 1

Copy the sentences below, completing each one with a phrase from the list.

1. Put the can _____
2. Put one square on the book and put _____
3. Light _____
4. Blow it _____
5. Put a cigarette in _____
6. Take _____
7. Draw a clock _____
8. Draw a fish _____
9. What's _____
10. Put the pencil in the _____

LIST

the other on the sofa.
out
in the purse.
smoking a cigarette.
out a match.
box.
your pocket.
showing five after six.
this?
the candle.

Exercise 2

Reorder the words below to form correct sentences.

1. candle light the
2. it blow out
3. show your me watch
4. my the matches put purse in
5. circle the touching touch I'm that
6. hair pull both hands with your
7. buttons count shirt the on brother's my
8. circle one touch point to the and other
9. draw glasses face and earrings sad a wearing
10 shake coin put can and in it the a

Lesson Summary

A	prepositions	**to** **after**	It's five **to** seven. It's five **after** seven.
B	pronoun **the other**		Put one circle on the floor and put **the other** on your hand.
C	**ing** phrases		Draw a clock, **showing five after eight.**

D	two-word verb **blow out**	**Blow out** the candle. **Blow** the candle **out.** **Blow** it **out.**
E	question words **where, what**	**Where's** the cat? **What's** this?

F information questions and long answers

Where are **you**?	**I'm** in back of the table.
Where are **John and Paul**?	**They're** in front of the desk.
Where's **Richard**?	**He's** next to the teacher.
Where's **Paula**?	**She's** in front of the window.
Where's the **cat**?	**It's** under the table.

G contractions (pronoun + Be)

I'm =	I + am
He's = **She's** = **It's** =	He + is She + is It + is
We're = **You're** = **They're** =	We + are You + are They + are

H contractions (question word + is)

Where's =	where + is
What's =	what + is

Vocabulary

after	he's	purse	we
am	I'm	she	we're
bag	light	she's	what
blow out	match	smoke (v)	what's
box	matches	the other	where
candle	match box	they	where's
cigarette	out	they're	
he	pocket	to	

99

LESSON SEVENTEEN

You will need

ball   book   bottle   candle   chair   eraser
flower   key   notebook   paper   pen   pencil   sponge

Key Sentences

Draw a picture to illustrate each Key Sentence.

1. Throw the ball into the air and catch it. **(Sample)**

2. Point to a friend.

3. Throw your friend the ball.

4. Tell your friend to throw it back.

5. Now throw the ball to your friend again.

6. Make a paper ball.

7. Throw it at the door.

8. Make another paper ball and throw it out the window.

9. Make a paper airplane.

10. Fly it to the window.

11. Fly around the room like a bird.

12. Squeeze the sponge.

13. Hand the sponge to a friend.

14. Hit someone on the head with the bottle.

15. Write the name of someone who isn't here with you now.

16. Write the names of two friends who aren't here with you now.

17. Draw a rectangle and divide it in half.

18. In the upper half draw a heart.

19. In the lower half draw a chair.

Participation Exercises

1.   Throw the

| ball |
| bottle |
| sponge |
| key |
| candle |

into the air and catch it.

2. Throw the

| ball |
| bottle |
| candle |
| sponge |
| notebook |

to a friend.

3. Throw me the

| ball |
| sponge |
| pen |
| pencil |
| eraser |

4. Hand the

| sponge |
| candle |
| flower |
| ball |
| eraser |

to a friend

5. Hit a friend on the head with the

| ball |
| book |
| notebook |
| sponge |
| candle |

7.

| Walk |
| Jump |
| Hop |
| Swim |

around the chair.

Now, do it again.

8. Draw a

| circle |
| square |
| triangle |
| rectangle |

and divide it in half.

Visual Practice Exercises

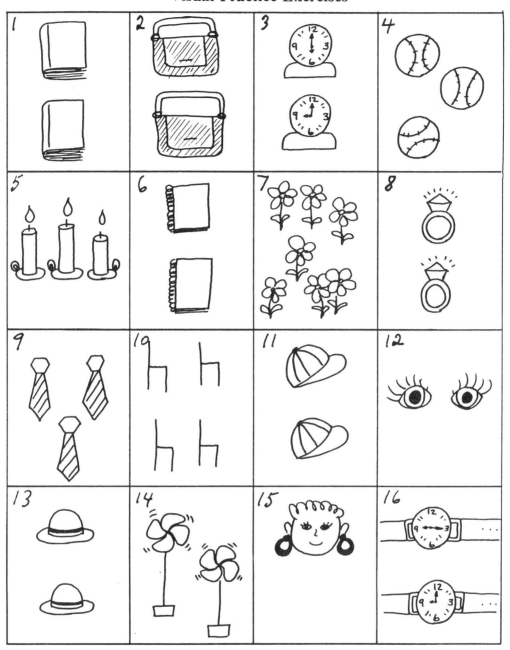

1. books	2. purses	3. clocks	4. balls
5. candles	6. notebooks	7. flowers	8. rings
9. ties	10. chairs	11. caps	12. eyes
13. hats	14. fans	15. earrings	16. watches

Ask and Answer

A	Are these **books?**

➡️

Yes, they are.
No, they aren't.

B	What are	these / those	?

➡️

They're **books**

103

Visual Practice Exercises

1. happy face	2. sad face	3. hand	4. foot
5. purse	6. airplane	7. flower	8. fish
9. eye	10. chair	11. crown	12. heart.

Drawing Activity: Close your book. Draw a rectangle and divide it in half with a horizontal line. Your partner will choose a rectangle from this page and use the directions below to tell you what to draw.

In the	upper half	draw a fish
	lower half	

Review and Reinforcement

Exercise 1

Copy the sentences below, filling in each blank with a word from the list.

1. _____ a paper ball.

2. Tell me the name of a friend who _____ here now.

3. Squeeze the _____ .

4. Hit me on the head _____ the bottle.

5. Draw a square and divide it in _____ .

6. _____ my hand.

7. Fly around the room _____ a bird.

8. _____ me the matches.

9. Throw the ball _____ the air.

10. Draw a circle in the _____ half.

LIST

isn't	sponge	half	some
squeeze	these	light	cough
into	with	like	hand
lower	pocket	make	

Exercise 2

Reorder the words below to form correct sentences.

1. airplane a make paper

2. a squeeze nose friend's

3. mother ball the throw your

4. throw a the to ball friend

5. draw divide half rectangle a and in it

6. window paper the the fly airplane to

7. back your friend ball the throw to

105

8. like room around an fly airplane the

9. me head with book the hit on a

10. name isn't write who here of the someone

Lesson Summary

A	preposition **at into**	Throw the ball **at** Pedro. Throw the ball **into** the air.
B	**noun** + noun **paper airplane** **paper ball**	Make a **paper airplane.** Throw the **paper ball** at the teacher.
C	demonstrative **these** **pronouns** **those**	**These** are books. **Those** are notebooks.

D yes/no questions and short answers

Are these books?		Yes, **they are.**
		No, **they aren't.**

E information questions and answers

What are	**these**	?		**They're** books.
	those			

F indirect object patterns with **throw**

Throw **your friend** the ball.
Throw the ball **to your friend.**

Vocabulary

again	divide	isn't	sponge
air	do	like	squeeze
at	fly	lower	these
back	half	make	those
ball	hand	paper airplane	throw
bottle	hit	paper ball	upper
catch	into		

106

LESSON EIGHTEEN

You will need

bottle of water   cup   desk   geometric figures (double set)
glass   paper   pencil   pitcher   table   towel

Key Sentences

Draw a picture to illustrate each Key Sentence.

1. Pick up the pitcher. **(Sample)**

2. Pour a little water into the cup.

3. Drink the water.

4. Hold the glass while a friend pours some water into it.

5. Pour a little water on one of your hands.

6. Show your wet hand to the class.

7. Point to your dry hand.

8. Pick up the towel and dry your wet hand.

9. Pour a little water on a friend's head.

10. Now pour some water on your own head.

11. Put your head on your desk and pretend you're sleeping.

12. Draw a rectangle.

13. In the center draw a happy face.

14. At the top draw a television.

15. At the bottom draw a cup.

16. Draw a diagonal line next to a horizontal line.

17. Draw a curved line under a vertical line.

107

Participation Exercises

1. Pick up both
    | triangles |
    | rectangles |
    | squares |
    | circles |

    Put down only one.
    Now put down the other.

2. Pour
    | some |
    | a little |
    water into the
    | cup |
    | glass |
    | bottle |

3. Pick up the towel and dry your
    | hands |
    | face |

4. Hold the
    | cup |
    | glass |
    | bottle |
    while a friend pours some water into it.

5. Draw a
    | horizontal |
    | vertical |
    | diagonal |
    | curved |
    line.

6. Add
    | 13 |
    | 14 |
    | 15 |
    | 16 |
    | 17 |
    | 18 |
    | 19 |
    | 20 |
    and
    | 4 |
    | 2 |
    | 6 |
    | 3 |
    | 5 |
    | 1 |
    | 7 |

7. Stand at the
    | door |
    | window |
    | table |
    | desk |

Visual Practice Exercises

1	2	3	4	5	6	7	8	9	10
11	12	13	14	15	16	17	18	19	20

one	two	three	four
five	six	seven	eight
nine	ten	eleven	twelve
thirteen	fourteen	fifteen	sixteen
seventeen	eighteen	nineteen	twenty

Listen and Perform

A	Touch Put the coin on Point to	number **5**		
B	Touch Put the coin on Point to	the number that comes	before / after	**8.**
C	Touch Put the coin on Point to	the number that comes between **14** and **16**		

Ask and Answer

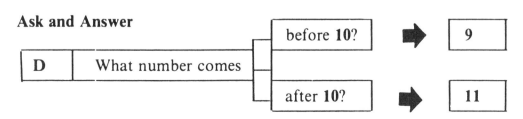

D	What number comes	before **10**? →	9
		after **10**? →	11

109

Visual Practice Exercises

airplane	bird	book	boy
cap	cat	chair	circle
crown	cup	door	eye
fan	fish	flower	girl
hand	happy face	hat	heart
sad face	square	table	television
tie	triangle	window	

Drawing Activity: Close your book and draw a big square. Your partner will choose a square from this page and use the directions below to tell you what to draw.

At the top In the center At the bottom	draw a door

Visual Practice Exercises

1. jumping	2. hopping	3. swimming	4. crying	5. laughing
6. running	7. praying	8. sleeping	9. stretching	10. singing

Listen and Perform

A	Touch Point to Count the letters in the name of Put the coin on	the student who's **jumping**.

Ask and Answer

B	Who's **crying**	➡	**Olivia** is.
C	What's **Stan** doing?	➡	**Praying.** He's **praying.** **Jumping.** She's **jumping.**
D	Is **Stan praying?**	➡	Yes, he is. No, he isn't. Yes, she is. No, she isn't.

Review and Reinforcement

Exercise 1

Copy the sentences below, filling in each blank with a word.

1. _____ a little water into the glass. (pour   give   drink)

2. Point to your _____ hand. (dry   hold   upper)

3. Pretend you're _____ . (sheep   again   sleeping)

4. Pour some water on your _____ head. (each   own   lower)

5. Draw a _____ line under a cat. (horizontal   candle   beard)

6. Pick up the _____ and dry your face. (towel   crown   watch)

7. Draw a window at the _____ . (center   bottom   skirt)

8. Draw an airplane between two _____ lines. (sad   but   curved)

9. _____ a little water. (shake   drink   another)

10. In the _____ , write your name. (ring   center   catch)

Exercise 2
Reorder the words below to form correct sentences.

1. you're pretend sleeping

2. a take match out

3. your me dry show hand

4. at name your bottom, the write

5. water glass some the pour into

6. sad center, in face a draw the a

7. pick your towel dry up the and hands

8. curved vertical two draw line lines a between

9. little own on pour a water your now head

10. I into water some hold it while the glass pour

Lesson Summary

A	preposition **at**	Stand **at** the door.
B	determiners **some** (with non-count nouns)	Pour **a little/some** water into the glass.
C	present tense (3rd person singular)	Hold the glass while a friend **pours** some water into it.
D	question word **what + number**	**What number** comes after ten?
E	subordinate conjunction **while**	Hold the cup **while** I pour you some coffee.
F	clauses: **while** **that**	Touch the number **that comes after eight.** Hold the glass **while I pour some water into it.**

G present continuous

I'm	
He's She's	**going** to school
We're You're They're	

H yes/no questions and short answers

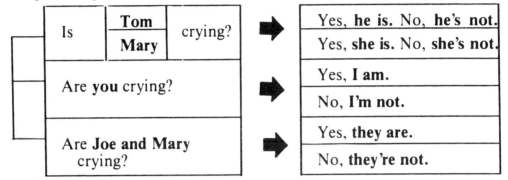

Is	Tom Mary	crying?	➡	Yes, **he is.** No, **he's not.** Yes, **she is.** No, **she's not.**
Are **you** crying?			➡	Yes, **I am.** No, **I'm not.**
Are **Joe and Mary** crying?			➡	Yes, **they are.** No, **they're not.**

I information questions and answers

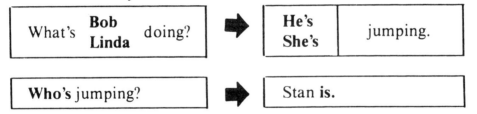

| What's | Bob
Linda | doing? | ➡ | He's
She's | jumping. |

| Who's jumping? | ➡ | Stan **is.** |

Vocabulary

at	diagonal	horizontal	school	twenty
a little	drink	line	seventeen	vertical
bottom	dry(v)	nineteen	sixteen	water
center	eighteen	own (adj)	sleep	wet
coffee	fifteen	pitcher	snore	while
cup	fourteen	pour	thirteen	
curved	glass	pours	towel	

LESSON NINETEEN

You will need

bell   chair   paper   pencil

Key Sentences

Draw a picture to illustrate each Key Sentence.

1. Walk backwards to the door. **(Sample)**

2. Ring the bell.

3. Stand up.

4. Turn right.

5. Raise your left hand.

6. Touch the four corners of the table.

7. Draw a big rectangle.

8. In the upper corners draw a triangle.

9. In the lower corners draw a circle.

10. Draw another rectangle.

11. In the right hand corners draw a heart.

12. In the left hand corners draw an eye.

13. Draw two clouds over a small house with three windows.
    It's raining.

14. Draw a small butterfly on the nose of a girl who's flying a kite.

15. Write the name of a friend who wasn't in class yesterday.

16. After you touch your nose, jump to the door.

17. Before you point to the ceiling, touch the floor.

Participation Exercises

1.
| Jump |
| Hop |
| Walk |
| Run |
| Swim |

around the chair backwards.

2. Ring the bell
| 2 |
| 4 |
| 6 |
| 8 |
| 10 |
times.

3. Turn
| around |
| right |
| left |

4. Raise your

right hand
left hand
hands

Put

it/them

down.

5. Draw a

circle
rectangle
triangle
square

with your

right hand
left hand

6. Draw a rectangle and draw a

circle
heart
hat
triangle

in the four corners.

7. Draw a rectangle.

In the

right hand
left hand

corners, draw a/an

eye
circle
triangle
heart

8. Draw a rectangle.

In the

upper
lower

corners, draw a

flower
fish
chair
hat

9. Draw a/an

airplane
butterfly
cloud
kite

over a house.

Visual Practice Exercises

Sunday
Monday
Tuesday
Wednesday
Thursday
Friday
Saturday

Listen and Perform

A	Touch Put the coin on Point to	the day that comes	before after	**Sunday.**

Ask and Answer

B	If today's **Monday,**	what day is tomorrow?	➡	**Tuesday**
		what day was yesterday?	➡	**Sunday**

C	What's on t.v. **Sunday** night?	_____

D	If today's **Tuesday, was yesterday Monday?**	Yes, it was. No, it wasn't.

Visual Practice Exercises

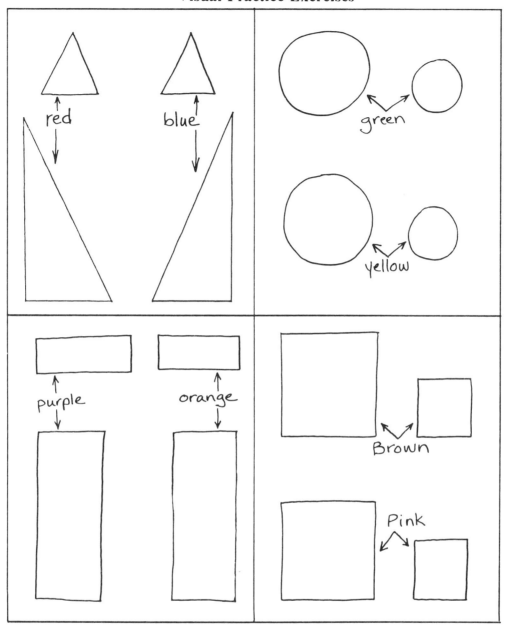

Guessing Game: Your partner chooses a figure from this page but doesn't tell you which one. Ask the questions below to discover the figure that was chosen.

	1	a circle	a triangle		?	
		a square	a rectangle			
						Yes, it is.
Is it	2	big		small	?	
						No, it isn't.
	3	red	blue	green yellow	?	
		purple	orange	brown pink		
	4	So it's the	Big	**red triangle.**		
			Small			

119

Review and Reinforcement

Exercise 1

Copy the sentences below, completing each one with something from the list.

1. In the right hand corners draw a _____

2. It's _____

3. What day _____ _____

4. Raise your _____

5. Turn _____

6. Draw a girl ringing _____

7. Draw a boy _____

8. Draw a house between _____

9. Jump around _____

10. If Sunday comes before Saturday, _____

LIST
left hand.
a bell.
raining.
right.
circle.
two trees.
comes after
   Monday?
pull your hair.
the class
   backwards.
flying a kite.

Exercise 2

Reorder the words below to form correct sentences

1. the ring bell

2. left raise hand your

3. two to people cry tell

4. backwards desk walk the around

5. ear chalkboard with an the touch

6. corners square draw a upper the in

7. corners paper this touch of the four

8. over small a a house draw cloud

9. flying girl who's kite touch a the

10. triangle, don't me pick the show up it to but

Lesson Summary

A	days of the week	**Sunday Thursday Monday Friday Tuesday Saturday Wednesday** — Today is **Monday.**
B	pronoun **it** (in impersonal (expressions)	**It's** raining.
C	present tense (3rd person singular)	Touch the day that **comes** after Friday.
D	prepositions **over under**	Write a number that's **over** seven but **under** ten.
E	past of be **(was)**	Yesterday **was** Tuesday.
F	question word **what** + **day**	**What day** is today?
G	noun + noun **Sunday night**	What's on t.v. **Sunday night?**
H	conjunctive adverb **so**	**So,** it's the big red triangle.
I	subordinate conjunctions **before after**	**After** you point to the door, cry. **Before** you touch your nose, laugh.
J	clauses **if that before after**	**If** today's Monday, what day is tomorrow? Touch the day **that** comes before Sunday. **After** you point to the door, cry. **Before** you touch your nose, laugh.

K contraction

wasn't = was + **not**

L yes/no questions and short answers

Is it a circle?

Yes **it is**
No, **it isn't**

M sentence pattern

In the	**right hand corners**	draw a circle.
	left hand corners	

N yes/no questions and short answers

Was yesterday Monday?

Yes, **it was.**
No, **it wasn't.**

Vocabulary

backwards	house	rain	Thursday
bell	it's	raise	today
butterfly	kite	right (turn right)	tomorrow
cloud	left (turn left)	right (right hand)	Tuesday
corner	left (left hand)	ring	was
day	Monday	Saturday	Wednesday
fly (a kite)	night	so	week
Friday	over	Sunday	what day
			yesterday

LESSON TWENTY

You will need

book   chair   geometric figures (simple set)   paper   pencil

Key Sentences

Draw a picture to illustrate each Key Sentence.

1. Draw a girl next to a tree, holding an umbrella. **(Sample)**

2. There's a cloud over her head and it's raining.

3. Draw an envelope over a shopping cart.

4. Draw something you see at an airport.

5. Draw something you see at a beach.

6. Draw something you see at a park.

7. Draw something you see at a post office.

8. Draw something you see at a supermarket.

9. Write the name of a bank.

10. Write the name of a drugstore.

11. Draw a big rectangle.

12. In the upper left hand corner draw a sad face.

13. In the lower right hand corner draw a flower.

14. In the upper right hand corner draw an airplane.

15. In the lower left hand corner draw a cloud.

16. Jump to a window and touch the window you jumped to.

17. Show a triangle to the class and then put the triangle you showed to the class on your head.

18. I'm going to say a number, either a number over ten or a number under ten.

19. If I say a number over ten, then you'll touch your nose, but if I say a number under ten, then you'll pull your hair.

Participation Exercises

1.
| Jump |
| Walk |
| Hop |
| Wave |
to a friend and touch the friend you
| jumped |
| walked |
| hopped |
| waved |
to.

2. Touch a friend and pull the
| hair |
| nose |
| ears |
of the friend you just touched.

3. Show a book to the class and then put the book you showed to the class

on	the chair.
under	
in front of	
in back of	
next to	

4. Turn your chair around and then

touch	the chair you turned around.
point to	
sit on	

5. Draw something you see at a/an

airport
beach
park
post office
supermarket

6. Draw a house. There's a

tree	next to it.
girl	
flower	
cat	

7. I'm going to say a number, either a number over ten or a number under ten. If I say a number over ten,

then you'll

Jump to the window
Hop to the door
Draw a circle
Tell me your name
Close the door

But if I say a number under ten,

then you'll

pull your hair
touch your nose
pick up the flower
open the door
stand next to the sofa

Visual Practice Exercises

1. park	2. beach	3. drugstore	4. bank
5. post office	6. supermarket	7. airport	8. theater

Listen and Perform

A	Touch Point to Tell me the name of the Whisper the name of Put the coin on	man boy woman girl	who's at the **park.**

Ask and Answer

B	Who's at the **park?**
C	Where's **Dan?**
D	Is **Dan** at the **park?**

Dan is.	
At the **park.**	He's at the **park.**
At the **bank.**	She's at the **bank.**
Yes, he is.	No, he's not.
Yes, she is.	No, she's not.

126

Visual Practice Exercises

airplane	bell	butterfly	candle
chair	circle	cloud	cup
door	eye	glass	happy face
hat	heart	house	kite
rectangle	sad face	square	television
tree	triangle	umbrella	window

Drawing Activity: Close your book and draw a big rectangle. Your partner will choose a rectangle from this page and use the directions below to tell you what to draw.

In the	upper	right hand corner	draw a **cloud.**
	lower	left hand corner	

127

Review and Reinforcement

Exercise 1
Copy the sentences below, filling in the blanks with words from the list.

1. Draw an envelope over a _____ cart.

2. Draw _____ you see at a park.

3. Write the name _____ a bank.

4. Touch the window you _____ to.

5. Give me the triangle you _____ to the class.

6. Draw a heart in the _____ left hand corner.

7. _____ a cloud over the tree.

8. Draw a kite in the lower _____ hand corner.

9. I'm going to draw _____ a pen or a cup.

10. If I draw a cat, you _____ tell me your name.

LIST

jumped	upper	something
shopping	was	either
day	will	cloud
night	butterfly	of
showed	right	there's

Exercise 2
Reorder the words below to form correct sentences.

1. ball the catch

2. up turn and stand left

3. draw between clouds butterfly two a

4. name bank write of the a

5. draw holding umbrella an girl a

6. I'm say number going a to

7. Monday, jump today's to if door the

8. tell beach me of a name the

9. something supermarket see a draw you at

10. corner, cat lower the in a draw hand left

Lesson Summary

A	places	**airport** **drugstore** **park** **post office** **beach** **theater** **supermarket** **bank**	Touch the man who's at the **bank.**
B	dummy subject **there** **(there's)**	**There's** a book on the table. Pick it up.
C	conjunction **either . . . or**	I'm going to draw **either** a circle **or** a triangle.
D	impersonal pronoun **you**	Draw something **you** see at the beach.
E	omission of relative pronoun **that**	Draw something **that** you see at a park.
F	**who** clauses	Touch the woman **who's** **at the beach.**

G   future with **going to**

I'm	
He's She's	**going to** draw some circles.
We're You're They're	

H   future with **will**

I You He She We They	**will close** the door.

I contractions (pronoun + will)

I'll	=	I	+	will
You'll	=	You	+	will
He'll	=	He	+	will
She'll	=	She	+	will
We'll	=	We	+	will
They'll	=	They	+	will

J yes/no questions and short answers

is **Bob** / **Sue** at the park?

Yes, **he is.**	No, **he's not.**
Yes, **she is.**	No, **she's not.**

K information questions and answers

Where's **Jack** / **Fran** ?

He's / She's at the supermarket.

L

Who's at the bank?

Pete **is.**

M sentence pattern

In the	**upper**	**right hand corner**	draw a door.
	lower	**left hand corner**	

N contraction

there's	=	there	+	is

O past tense

base form	Past
show	**showed**
jump	**jumped**

Vocabulary

airport	he'll	she'll	tree
bank	I'll	shopping cart	umbrella
beach	just	supermarket	under
drugstore	over	theater	we'll
either . . . or	park	there	will
envelope	post office	there's	you'll
going to	see	they'll	

LESSON TWENTY-ONE

You will need

chair   paper   pencil

Key Sentences

Draw a picture to illustrate each Key Sentence.

1. Draw a fat man with long hair. **(Sample)**

2. Draw a thin man with a beard.

3. Draw a short man with a long neck.

4. Draw a tall man with a beard and a mustache.

5. Draw an upside-down house between two big butterflies.

6. Draw three short vertical lines over a long horizontal line.

7. Draw the sun between the moon and a star.

8. Draw a few circles.

9. Draw many small triangles.

10. Jump to this chair over here.

11. Hop to that chair over there.

12. Pull someone's hair and then touch the nose of the person whose hair you pulled.

13. Wave to a friend and then say "hello" to the person you waved to.

Participation Exercises

1. Draw a | long <br> short | vertical <br> diagonal <br> horizontal <br> curved | line.

2. Draw a | fat man <br> thin man | with | long hair <br> short hair <br> big eyes <br> small feet |

3. Draw a | tall man <br> short man | with a | beard <br> mustache <br> long neck <br> big mouth |

4. Draw an upside-down | airplane <br> house <br> butterfly <br> girl |

5. Draw | a star <br> the sun <br> the moon | over a/an | airplane <br> tree <br> house |

6. Draw | a few <br> many | circles <br> triangles <br> stars <br> hearts <br> eyes |

7. Squeeze a friend's hand and then | touch <br> point to <br> pull the hair of |

the friend whose hand you squeezed.

132

Visual Practice Exercises

1. park	2. beach	3. drugstore	4. bank
5. post office	6. supermarket	7. airport	8. theater

Listen and Perform

A	Touch Put the coin on Whisper the names of Point to	the women who were at the **park.**

Ask and Answer

B	Were **Kate** and **Lillian** at the **park?**		Yes, they were. No, they weren't.

Visual Practice Exercises

airplane	ball	beard	bell	between
bird	butterfly	button	cap	cat
chair	circle	clock	cloud	crown
cup	curved	diagonal	door	ear
envelope	eye	fan	fat	fish
flower	foot	girl	glass	hair
hand	happy	hat	heart	horizontal
house	in	key	kite	line
ring	sad	short	small	square
star	sun	table	television	tie
tree	triangle	umbrella	upside-down	vertical
window	with			

Drawing Activity: Close your book and draw a big rectangle. Your partner will choose a rectangle from this page and using the model sentences below, will tell you what to draw.

In the center At the top At the bottom	draw a _____

In the	upper	right hand corner	draw a _____
	lower	left hand corner	

Next to the	on the left	draw a _____
	on the right	

134

Guessing Game: Your partner chooses a figure from this page, but doesn't tell you which one. Ask the questions below to discover the figure that was chosen.

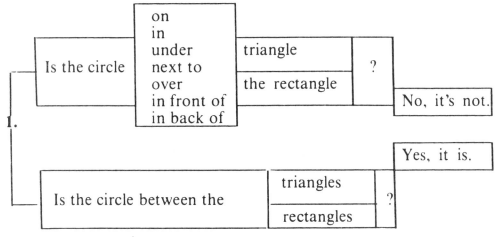

Review and Reinforcement

Exercise 1

Copy the sentences below, filling in the blanks.

1. Hop to that chair _____ there. (over   under   see)

2. Draw a _____ vertical line. (there's   tree   long)

3. Draw an _____ airplane. (upside-down   umbrella going to)

4. Draw a _____ small circles. (few   many   rain)

5. Draw a tall _____ man. (kite   thin   left)

6. Touch the person _____ hair you pulled. (who   that whose

7. Say "hello" to the person you _____ to. (raise   waved bell)

8. Swim to _____ chair over here. (these   this   that)

9. Draw the sun next to a _____ . (was   star   day)

10. Draw _____ small triangles. (glass   wet   many)

Exercise 2
Reorder the words below to form correct sentences

1. many circles small draw

2. triangles a big draw few

3. short lines three draw vertical

4. man draw thin a tall

5. hop over that to there student

6. person to touch waved the you

7. man tie draw a wearing a fat

8. man with short a a draw beard

9. upside-down two between an triangles butterfly draw

10. point pulled person you hair the to whose

Lesson Summary

A	adjectives **fat** **thin** **tall** **short**	Draw a **fat** man.
B	adjective phrases	Draw a tall man **with long hair.**
C	conjunctive adverb **then**	**Then** you chose that one.
D	past of be **were**	Write the names of two friends who **were** in class yesterday.
E	indefinite determiners **a few/many**	Draw **many** small circles around **a few** triangles.
F	relative pronoun **whose**	Point to the person **whose** hair you pulled.
G	clauses **who** **whose**	Touch the women **who were at the park.** Shake hands with the person **whose hair you pulled.**

H yes / no questions (with is) and short answers

Is the circle on the triangle?

Yes, **it is.**
No, **it's not.**

I yes / no questions (with were) and short answers

Were Paul and Joe at the park?

Yes, they were.
No, they weren't.

J past tense (regular)

base form	past
wave	**waved**
pull	**pulled**

K past tense (irregular)

base form	past
choose	**chose**

L contraction

weren't = were + not

M irregular plural

singular	plural
woman	**women**

Vocabulary

choose	over here	tall	weren't
chose	over there	then	whose
fat	short	thin	women
long	star	upside-down	
moon	sun	were	

LESSON TWENTY-TWO

You will need

bottle of	chair	glass	scissors	table
bowl	cup	pail	sofa	television

Key Sentences

Draw a picture to illustrate each Key Sentence.

1. Draw a circle with broken lines. **(Sample)**

2. Draw a long broken horizontal line next to a short vertical line.

3. Draw a happy face with a circle for its nose.

4. Draw an arrow through a heart.

5. Add the numbers ten and seventeen and then draw a triangle around the sum of the numbers you added.

6. Touch someone's nose and then point to the person whose nose you touched.

7. Face the door and point to the door you're facing.

8. Kick the wall and then touch the wall you kicked.

9. Pour a little bit of water into the bowl.

10. Pour a lot of water into the pail.

11. Pick up the scissors and cut your hair.

Participation Exercises

1.   Face the

wall
window
television
sofa
door

2.   Kick the

wall
door
sofa
table
chair

3. Pour | a little / a lot of | water into the | bowl / pail / cup / glass |

4. Pull a friend's | nose / hair / ears | and then shake hands

with the person whose nose you pulled.

5. Draw a | circle / square / triangle / rectangle | with broken lines.

6. Draw a | long / short | broken | horizontal / curved / diagonal / vertical | line

7. Add the numbers | 11 / 15 / 13 / 18 / 20 | and | 5 / 8 / 3 / 14 / 19 |

and draw a | circle / triangle / square / rectangle | around the sum of the numbers you added.

8. Draw an arrow | pointing to / through | a | heart / fat man / tree / circle / hat |

141

Visual Practice Exercises

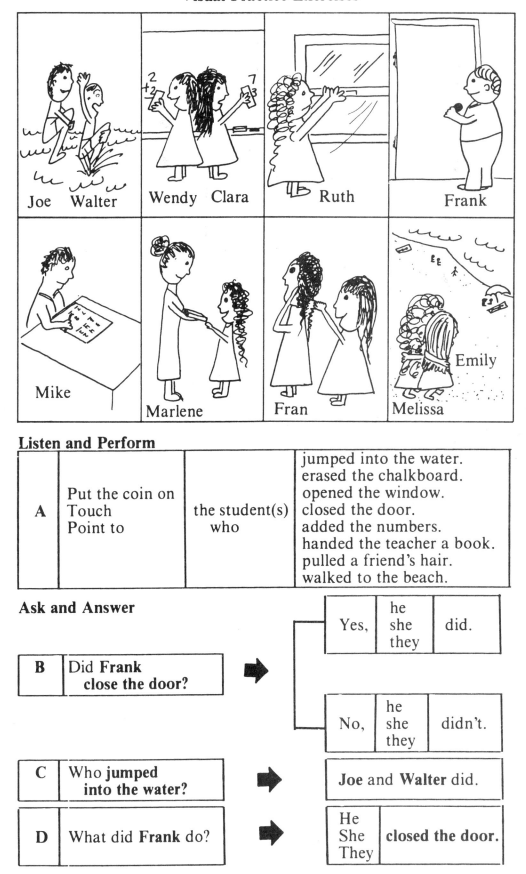

Joe   Walter   Wendy   Clara   Ruth   Frank

Mike   Marlene   Fran   Melissa   Emily

Listen and Perform

A	Put the coin on Touch Point to	the student(s) who	jumped into the water. erased the chalkboard. opened the window. closed the door. added the numbers. handed the teacher a book. pulled a friend's hair. walked to the beach.

Ask and Answer

B	Did **Frank** **close the door?**

Yes,	he she they	did.

No,	he she they	didn't.

C	Who **jumped** **into the water?**

Joe and **Walter** did.

D	What did **Frank** do?

He She They	**closed the door.**

142

Visual Practice Exercises

Joel Jack Pete Gil

Jeff Sam Ted Steve

Guessing Game: Your partner chooses a figure from this page, but doesn't tell you which one. Ask the questions below to discover the figure that was chosen.

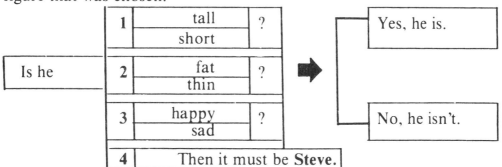

Is he	1	tall	?	→	Yes, he is.
		short			
	2	fat	?		
		thin			
	3	happy	?		No, he isn't.
		sad			
	4	Then it must be **Steve.**			

Note: You can also use these expression:
It can't be Jack because he's tall.
It could be Sam because he's short.

Visual Practice Exercises

add	a few	airplane	arrow	beard
bell	big	broken	butterfly	button
cat	chair	circle	clock	cloud
crown	curved	diagonal	door	ear
envelope	eye	face	fan	fat
fish	flower	forehead	girl	glasses
hair	hand	happy	head	heart
holding	horizontal	house	key	kite
line	long	man	many	moon
mustache	nose	pocket	pointing to	rectangle
sad	scissors	short	small	square
star	sum	sun	table	television
tree	triangle	umbrella	upside-down	vertical
wearing	window			

Drawing Activity: Close your book and draw a big rectangle. Your partner will choose a rectangle from this page and using the words below, will tell you what to draw.

in the upper-lower/right-left hand corner			
in the center	at the top	at the bottom	next to
on the right	on the left	from . . .to	between
in	on	under	over
in front of	in back of	around	with
through	for	there's	

144

A. Drawing Activity: Cover the drawing on this page. Take out a sheet of paper and draw a big rectangle. **Read the sentences below and draw.**

1. In the center, draw a fat man with long hair, wearing a hat and a tie.

2. In the upper left hand corner, there's an upside-down butterfly with a circle around it.

3. At the top, draw an airplane.

4. In front of this airplane, draw a happy face with a long nose and triangles for eyes.

5. Draw an arrow through the hat that the fat man is wearing.

6. This fat man has a kite in one hand and he's holding an umbrella in the other.

7. Next to the fat man, on the left, draw a girl with only one eye, standing on a chair.

8. Over the umbrella that the fat man is holding, draw a cloud between two stars.

9. At the bottom, draw a sad face with one big ear and one small ear.

10. In the lower left hand corner, there's a tree with the sun over it.

11. Next to the fat man, on the right, draw a heart with broken lines.

12. Draw a diagonal line from the heart to the sad face at the bottom.

13. There's a fish with a house on its head in the lower right hand corner.

14. Between the fish and the sad face draw many small circles around a few small triangles.

15. In the upper right hand corner draw a heart and under this heart put a tall thin man with a big mustache.

B. Drawing Activity: cover the sentences on this page. Look at the picture and **tell your partner what to draw.**

145

Review and Reinforcement

Exercise 1

Copy the sentences below, completing each one with a phrase from the list.

1. Draw a long _____

2. Draw a circle around the sum _____

3. Point to the person whose _____

4. Point to the person _____.

5. Touch the wall _____

6. Pour a little bit _____

7. Pick up the scissors and _____

8. Draw an arrow _____

9. Pour a lot of _____

10. It can't be Albert _____

LIST

water into the pail
nose you pulled.
because he's short.
cut your hair.
you're facing
broken horizontal line.
through a heart.
kicked.
of the numbers you added.
of water into the cup.

Exercise 2

Reorder the words below to form correct sentences.

1. both raise hands

2. head shake times your two

3. wet point hand to your

4. line long horizontal a draw broken

5. sponge hands both the with squeeze

6. fat arrow through an a draw man

7. cut scissors hair up my the and pick

8. into bit cup pour the water of little a

9. facing touch window window face a the you're and

10. for sad nose a triangle a with face draw its

Vocabulary

a lot of	bowl	did	must be
arrow	broken (line)	didn't	pail
be	can't be	face	scissors
because	could be	for	through
bit	cut	kick	

Lesson Summary

A	indefinite determiner **a lot of** (with non-count nouns)	Pour **a lot of** water into the glass.
B	prepositions **through** **for**	Draw an arrow **through** a heart. Draw a happy face with a circle **for** its nose.
C	Models **can't** be (impossibility) **could** be (possibility) **must** be (conclusion)	It **can't** be Pedro. It **could** be Roberto. It **must** be Jose.
D	Clauses **because** **whose**	It can't be Pedro **because he's short.** Touch someone's nose and point to the person **whose nose you touched.**

E yes/no questons (with did) and short answers

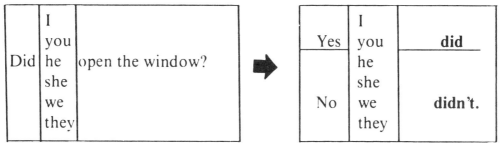

F past tense

I You He She We They	**added** the numbers.

G contraction

didn't = did + not

H yes/no questions (with is) and short answers

147

LESSON TWENTY-THREE

You will need

book   comic book   magazine   notebook   pencil   table

chair   glass   newspaper   paper   sofa

Key Sentences

Draw a picture to illustrate each Key Sentence.

1. Open the book to page ten and read. **(Sample)**

2. Hold the newspaper upside down.

3. Hit someone on the head with the comic book.

4. Hand the magazine to a friend.

5. Sit on the floor and pray.

6. Draw a church next to a house.

7. Draw ten triangles in a row.

8. Draw a circle around one and a rectangle around the others.

9. Draw five eyes in a column.

10. Draw a bookcase with three shelves.

11. Draw some books on the middle shelf.

12. Draw a lamp on the shelf above the books.

13. Draw a clock on the shelf below the books.

148

Participation Exercises

1. Sit on the

    | sofa |
    | floor |
    | chair |
    | table |

    and pray.

2. Open the

    | book |
    | comic |
    | magazine |
    | newspaper |

    to page

    | 5 |
    | 8 |
    | 4 |
    | 10 |

    and read.

3. Hold the

    | book |
    | comic |
    | magazine |
    | newspaper |
    | glass |

    upside down.

4. Hit a friend on the head with the

    | magazine |
    | book |
    | newspaper |
    | comic |
    | notebook |

5. Draw

    | 5 |
    | 6 |
    | 7 |
    | 8 |

    | hats |
    | hearts |
    | flowers |

    in a row.

    Draw a circle around one and a rectangle around the others.

6. Draw a bookcase with three shelves and draw a lamp on the middle shelf.

    On the shelf

    | above |
    | below |

    the lamp, draw a

    | clock |
    | cat |
    | key |
    | fish |
    | scissors |

Visual Practice Exercises

2	12	20
3	13	30
4	14	40
5	15	50
6	16	60
7	17	70
8	18	80
9	19	90

1	one
2	two
3	three
4	four
5	five
6	six
7	seven
8	eight
9	nine
10	ten
11	eleven
12	twelve
13	thirteen
14	fourteen
15	fifteen
16	sixteen
17	seventeen
18	eighteen
19	nineteen
20	twenty
21	twenty-one
22	twenty-two
23	twenty-three
24	twenty-four
25	twenty-five
26	twenty-six
27	twenty-seven
28	twenty-eight
29	twenty-nine
30	thirty
40	forty
50	fifty
60	sixty
70	seventy
80	eighty
90	ninety
100	one hundred

Listen and Repeat

	two	twelve	twenty
	three	thirteen	thirty
	four	fourteen	forty
A	five	fifteen	fifty
	six	sixteen	sixty
	seven	seventeen	seventy
	eight	eighteen	eighty
	nine	nineteen	ninety

Listen and Perform

B	Touch Put the coin on **Point to**	number **20.**

Visual Practice Exercises

Guessing Game: Your partner chooses a person in the picture but doesn't tell you which one. Ask the questions below to discover the person who was chosen.

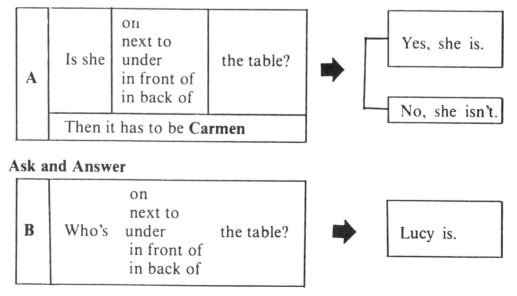

Ask and Answer

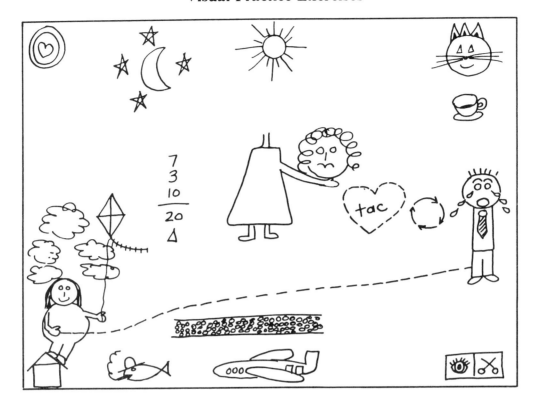

A. **Drawing Activity:** Cover the drawing on this page. Take out a sheet of paper and draw a big rectangle. **Read the sentences below and draw.**

1. In the center, draw a girl holding her head in her hand.

2. In the lower left hand corner, draw a fat man with long hair, standing on a house, flying a kite.

3. If Monday comes after Sunday, draw the sun at the top. But if it comes before Sunday, draw the moon in the lower left hand corner.

4. At the bottom, there's an airplane with three windows and two doors. This airplane is facing the lower left hand corner.

5. In the lower right hand corner, draw a rectangle and divide it in half with a vertical line.

6. In one half draw an eye, and in the other, put a scissors.

7. In the upper left hand corner, draw a heart and then draw two circles around it.

8. In front of the airplane there's a fish wearing a hat and smoking a cigarette.

9. Next to the girl without a head, on the left, add the numbers seven, three, and ten and then draw a triangle under the sum.

10. In the upper right hand corner, there's a cat with three ears. It has triangles for eyes.

11. Next to the girl, on the right, draw a heart with broken lines.

12. Above the airplane draw many small circles between two long horizontal lines.

13. Between the cat and the rectangle, there's a boy who is crying.

14. This boy is wearing a tie.

15. Between the boy and the heart, draw a circle with four curved arrows.

16. Draw some clouds over the fat man.

17. Next to the sun, on the left, draw the moon between four stars, one above, one below, one on the left, and one on the right.

18. If the sum of eight and seventeen is thirty-five, draw a button in back of the airplane. But if it isn't, then draw a cup under the cat.

19. Draw a broken line from the fat man's hand that isn't holding the kite to the boy who's crying.

20. There's an animal in the upper right hand corner. Write the name of this animal backwards in the heart that's next to the girl.

B. **Drawing Activity:** Cover the sentences on this page. **Look at the picture** and **tell your partner what to draw.**

Review and Reinforcement

Exercise 1

Copy the sentences below, filling in the blanks with words from the list.

1. Sit on the sofa and _____ .

2. Hold the book _____ in front of your face.

3. Draw a church next _____ a house.

4. Draw six hearts in a _____ .

5. Draw a bookcase with three _____ .

153

6. Draw some books on the middle _____ .

7. Give me one and put the _____ on the table.

8. My friend is reading a _____ .

9. It _____ be Linda because she's short.

10. Tell me the names of two friends who _____ here yesterday.

LIST

upside-down	must	shelves
moon	whose	others
shelf	pray	row
thin	women	weren't
to	will	magazine

Exercise 2
Reorder the words below to form correct sentences

1. me kick ball the

2. be must it Steve

3. seven draw row a hearts in

4. clock desk above draw a a

5. sit pray sofa and the on

6. bowl table the the on put

7. magazine read me open to and the

8. me name book a tell of the

9. jump window going to to the he's

10. draw one rectangle others circle and around the a a

Lesson Summary

A	prepositions **above below**	Put a book on the shelf **above** the clock. Put a glass on the shelf **below** the clock.
B	modal **has to** be	Then it **has to** be Carla
C	pronoun **the others**	Draw five flowers in a row. Erase one and draw a circle around **the others.**
D	numbers **21 — 100**	Add **twenty-five** and **thirty.**

E   yes/no questions and short answers

Is she in front of the table?

Yes, **she is.**
No, **she isn't.**

F   information questions and answers

Who's next to the table?

Rose **is.**

G   irregular plural

singular	plural
shelf	**shelves**

Vocabulary

above	fifty	newspaper	seventy
below	forty	ninety	shelf
bookcase	has to be	page	shelves
church	hundred	pray	sixty
column	lamp	read	the others
comic book	magazine	row	thirty
eighty	middle		

LESSON TWENTY-FOUR

You will need

bag	bowl	fan	newspaper	pen
ball	can	flower	notebook	pencil
book	car	glass	paper	sponge
bottle	comic book	key	pencil	table
bottle caps	cup	magazine	pail	television

Key Sentences

Draw a picture to illustrate each Key Sentence.

1. Shake hands with a friend and then tell me the name of the person you shook hands with. **(Sample)**

2. Swim to someone and then pull the nose of the person you swam to.

3. Run to the door and then open the door you ran to.

4. Draw a circle and then erase the circle you drew.

5. Give the flower to a friend and then hit the person you gave the flower to on the head with the bottle.

6. Throw the ball to someone and then whisper the name of the person you threw the ball to.

7. Drink a cup of coffee and then put the cup you drank the coffee in next to the glass.

8. Sing a song and then write the name of the song you sang.

9. Open the can and take out five bottle caps.

10. Drop them into the bowl one by one.

11. Pull a friend to the door.

12. Push someone to the T.V.

13. Drive the car to the door.

14. Honk the horn when you get there.

15. Draw three men swimming in a river.

16. Draw a bridge across the river.

Participation Exercises

1. Drop the

book
magazine
notebook
key
sponge

on the floor.

2. Open the can and take out

5
6
7
8

bottle caps.

Drop them into the

glass
bag
pail
cup
bowl

one by one.
one at a time.

3. | Push
 Pull | a friend to the | door <br> window
 t.v.
 fan <br> table |

4. Put the pen | on <br> in <br> under <br> in front of <br> in back of <br> next to | the glass.

5. Drive the car to the | door <br> window <br> fan <br> table |

Honk the horn when you get there.

6. Run to a friend and then | shake hands with <br> pull the ears of <br> give the flower <br> point to |

the person you ran to.

7. Give the | flower <br> book <br> pen <br> comic <br> newspaper | to a friend and

then | hit <br> say "hello" to <br> walk around <br> pull the hair of | the person you gave it to.

Visual Practice Exercises

Henry

Joyce

Bruce

Tom

Linda

Frank

Diana

Joel

Elaine   Mindy

Listen and Perform

| A | Put the coin on
Touch
Point to | the student(s)
who | shook hands with a
    friend.
swam in the river.
ran around the park.
drew a house on the
    chalkboard.
gave his teacher a flower.
threw the ball to a friend.
drank a cup of coffee.
sang some songs. |

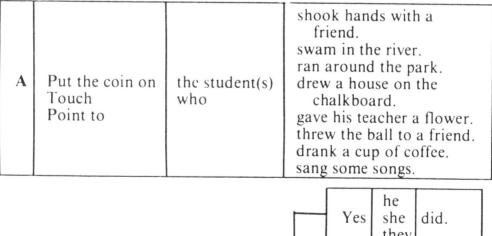

| B | Did **Joel drink** a cup of coffee? | ⟹ | Yes | he
she
they | did. |
| | | | No | he
she
they | didn't. |

| C | Who **swam** in the river? | ⟹ | **Joyce** did. |

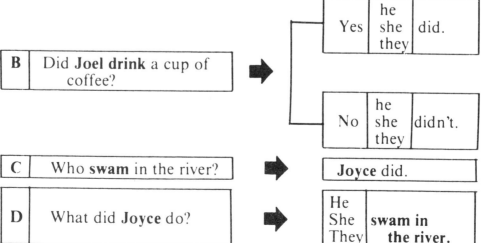

| D | What did **Joyce** do? | ⟹ | He
She
They | **swam in
the river.** |

159

Visual Practice Exercises

Dan   Alan   Max   Ben   Bob   Ted   Ken   Alex

Simon   Phil   Saul   Hugh   Leo   Ron   Albert   Darrel

Guessing Game: Your partner chooses a figure from this page, but doesn't tell you which one. **Ask the questions below to discover the figure that was chosen.**

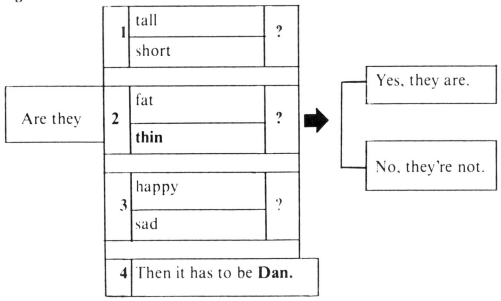

| | 1 | tall | ? |
| | | short | |

| Are they | 2 | fat | ? |
| | | **thin** | |

Yes, they are.

No, they're not.

| | 3 | happy | ? |
| | | sad | |

| | 4 | Then it has to be **Dan.** | |

Note: You can also use these expressions:

It can't be Dan and Alan because they're tall.

It could be Leo and Ron because they're short.

160

Visual Practice Exercises

A. **Drawing Activity:** Cover the drawing on this page. Take out a sheet of paper and draw a big rectangle. **Read the sentences below and draw.**

1. In the center draw a happy face with short hair, a long beard, and small eyes.

2. This happy face doesn't have any ears but has two teeth.

3. There's a church with two doors in the lower left hand corner.

4. In the upper left hand corner, draw an upside-down car.

5. At the top there's a butterfly with five short horizontal lines under it.

6. In the lower right hand corner, draw a fat man with two flowers in his pocket.

7. At the bottom, there's a river with two men swimming it it.

8. Look at the lower left hand corner. If you drew a car there, then draw a television next to the happy face, on the left. But if you drew a church there, then draw a television in the upper right hand corner.

9. Under the happy face with the two teeth, draw a lot of small triangles, and then draw a rectangle around them.

10. Between the church and the car, draw a ball and then draw another one below the television.

11. Next to the happy face, on the right, draw a row of seven circles.

12. Draw a square around one, and a broken horizontal line above the others.

13. Next to the happy face, on the left, there's a tall thin man with a big head, a big mustache, and a circle for his mouth.

14. He's wearing a crown and has a lamp in one hand, and a clock in the other.

15. If the tall thin man has something in both of his hands, put the number that comes after eighteen under the car. But if he doesn't have anything in one of his hands, then draw a triangle next to the television.

16. Draw a bridge across the river.

17. Between the fat man and the row of circles, draw a big sad face with a heart on each cheek.

18. Over the church, draw a cloud. There are two arrows through the cloud, one pointing up and the other pointing down.

19. Between the car and the butterfly, draw two men shaking hands.

20. The tall thin man isn't smoking a cigarette, but the sad face is.

B. Drawing Activity: Cover the sentences on this page. **Look at the picture and tell your partner what to draw.**

Review and Reinforcement

Exercise 1

Copy the sentences below, filling in each blank with a word.

1. Tell me the name of the song you _____ . (get   horn   sang)

2. _____ the car around the class. (lamp   drive   middle)

3. Erase the circle you _____ . (page   drew   hundred)

4. Touch the person you _____ the ball to (hold   above   threw

162

5. Hit the person who _____ the coffee on the head. (drank pour   pail)

6. Open the door you _____ to. (was   ran   through)

7. Drop the coins on the floor one at a _____ . (day time   whose

8. _____ a friend to the window. (make   go   push)

9. Draw a girl swimming in a _____ . (river   bridge across)

10. Pull the hair of the man who _____ hands with you. (do shook   give)

Exercise 2
Reorder the words below to form correct sentences.

1. drew erase you circle the

2. me to push chalkboard the

3. pull door sister the your to

4. car class drive around the the

5. open to window you the ran

6. be brother your it to has

7. men river two draw swimming in a

8. floor one drop one them by the on

9. person gave to flower the you the touch

10. song name me you sang tell of the the

Lesson Summary

A	noun + noun **bottle cap**	Take two **bottle caps** out of the can.
B	contrast **pull/push**	**Pull/Push** me to the door.
C	modal **has to** be	Then it **has to** be Pedro.

D   yes/no questions and short answers

Are they tall?

Yes, **they are.**
No, **they aren't.**

E   irregular past tense

base form	past
drink	**drank**
draw	**drew**
give	**gave**
run	**ran**
sing	**sang**
shake	**shook**
swim	**swam**
throw	**threw**

F   irregular plural

singular	plural
man	**men**

Vocabulary

across	drew	horn	river
anything	drive	men	sang
bottle cap	drop	one at a time	shook
bridge	gave	one by one	swam
car	get	push	there
drank	honk	ran	threw

LESSON TWENTY-FIVE

You will need

ball	flower	notebook	scissors
bell	magazine	paper	towel
book	matches	pencil	
bottle	newspaper	purse	

Key Sentences

Draw a picture to illustrate each Key Sentence.

1. Say "hello" to a friend and shake hands with the friend you said "hello" to. **(Sample)**

2. Write the name of an animal and then draw a circle around the name you wrote.

3. Make a paper airplane and then fly the airplane you made.

4. Tell someone to jump and then point to the person you told to jump.

5. Ring the bell and put the bell you rang in the purse.

6. Put the book on the floor and then cover the book you put on the floor with the towel.

7. Hit someone on the head with the bottle and then shake hands with the person you hit on the head.

8. Take out a match and then light the match you took out.

165

9. Blow out the match you lit.

10. Put the match you blew out in your pocket.

11. Tell a friend to sit down and then stoop in front of the person who sat down.

12. Cut a friends hair and point to the person whose hair you cut.

13. Draw a short boy next to a tall boy. Make the short boy's eyes bigger than the tall boy's.

14. Write a number that's more than twenty but less than thirty.

15. Draw a mountain surrounded by clouds.

16. In a column write the name of a country, a state, and an important city.

Participation Exercises

1.   Shake someone and then pull the

hair
nose
ears

of the person you shook.

2.   Swim to a friend and then

say
whisper

"hello" to the person you swam to.

3.   Tell someone to

jump
hop
cry
stoop
sing

and then throw the ball to the person you told to jump.

4. Put the book on the floor and cover the book you put on the floor with

    the

newspaper
magazine
towel

5. Hit someone on the head with the newspaper and then

shake hands with
say "hello" to
stand on the feet of

    the person you hit on the head.

6. Say "hello" to a friend and then

wave to
walk around
hop around
give the flower to

    the person you said "hello" to.

7. Draw a

heart
hat
cat
tree

    and then draw

a star
the sun
the moon

    over what you drew.

8. Write the name of a

city
country
state
river
mountain

    in the notebook and then

    draw a

circle
square
triangle
rectangle

    around the name you wrote.

Visual Practice Exercises

1	2	3	4
○ black ○ brown	△ green △ blue	□ gray □ purple	✿ yellow ✿ orange

5	6	7	8
♡ pink ♡ red	⌂ white ⌂ blue	🚗 orange 🚗 brown	🎩 purple 🎩 green

1. circle	2. triangle	3. square	4. flower
5. heart	6. house	7. car	8. hat

Listen and Perform

A	Touch the Put the coin on the Point to the	bigger	**circle.**
		smaller	

B	Which **triangle** is	bigger	?	➡	The **blue** one.
		smaller			

168

Visual Practice Exercises

Listen and Perform

A	Touch Point to Put the coin on	the student(s) who	said hello to the teacher. stood in line at the theater. for two hours. wrote a letter to a friend. read the newspaper. lit the candle. made a paper airplane. told a friend to jump. rang the bell.

Ask and Answer

B	Did **Stan ring the bell?**

	he she they	
Yes		did.

	he she they	
No		didn't.

C	Who **lit the candle?**

Denny did.

D	What did **Lucy** do?

He She They	**made a paper airplane**

169

A. **Drawing Activity:** Cover the drawing on this page. Take out a sheet of paper and draw a big rectangle. **Read the sentences below and draw.**

1. In the center, draw a fat man with his eyes closed. He has a triangle for his nose and his mouth is open in a circle.

2. Put both of his hands on his head and make one of his legs long and the other one short.

3. He's wearing a tie and there's a flower in his pocket.

4. At the bottom there's a short thin man pushing a car. The car and the man are facing the lower left hand corner.

5. In the upper left hand corner, add the numbers twenty-five, eight and two, and put a triangle around the sum.

6. If the sum of the numbers you added is more than thirty-seven, then put it under the fat man and draw a rectangle around it. But if it is less than thirty-seven, then you will draw a row of five circles at the top.

7. Next to the fat man, on the right, there's a tall woman who's holding a pitcher over his head and pouring some water on his head.

8. Draw the sun in the lower left hand corner, and then write the name of what you drew under the woman.

170

9. Next to the fat man, on the left, draw an upside-down house.

10. Between the sun and the numbers you added, draw a happy face.

11. This happy face has a long nose with a butterfly on it.

12. This happy face has long hair, two necks, and is wearing glasses.

13. There's a cloud over the woman's head and it's raining.

14. In back of the woman draw a column of six hearts.

15. Draw a circle around one of the hearts and a rectangle around the others.

16. In the lower right hand corner, draw a clock showing five after eight.

17. Next to this clock, draw a girl with only one leg. She's holding a fish in one hand and is flying a kite with the other. The kite is over the clock.

18. Under the fat man, draw a sad face between two broken vertical lines. This sad face has short hair, a beard and a big mustache.

19. In the upper right hand corner, draw a cat smoking a cigarette.

20. Draw two arrows, one pointing to the woman, and the other through her.

B. **Drawing Activity:** Cover the sentences on pages 170 and 171. **Look at the picture and tell your partner what to draw.**

Review and Reinforcement

Exercise 1

Copy the sentences below, completing each one with a phrase from the list.

1. Shake hands with the person you said _____

2. Fly the airplane _____

3. Draw a mountain _____

4. Show me the bell that _____

5. Light the _____

6. Blow out the match _____

7. Make the short boy's _____

8. Point to the person _____

9. Paris is _____

10. Write a number that's _____

LIST

that you made.
you rang.
that you lit.
eyes bigger.
"hello" to.
an important city.
match you took out.
more than fifty.
whose hair you cut.
surrounded by clouds.

171

Exercise 2

Reorder the words below to form correct sentences

1. match lit out the blow you

2. man's bigger the eyes make tall

3. person down who the sat touch

4. that paper made fly airplane you the

5. paper me took you give the out

6. hair whose touch cut person the you

7. bell person who the touch the rang

8. rectangle wrote draw you around a name the

9. point you sit to down told to the person

10. hit head point the on person you the to

Lesson Summary

A	pronoun **one**	Give me the small **one**.
B	question word **which**	**Which** circle is smaller?
C	preposition **by**	Draw a mountain surrounded by **by** clouds.
D	relative pronoun **what**	Do something and then tell me **what** you did.
E	clauses **what** **whose**	Draw something and then tell **what you drew.** Kick the person **whose nose you pulled.**

F information questions and answers

Which triangle is bigger?

The blue one.

G irregular past tense (past same as present)

base form	Past
hit	**hit**
put	**put**

H irregular past tense (with vowel change)

base form	past
blow out	**blew out**
light	**lit**
make	**made**
ring	**rang**
say	**said**
sit	**sat**
tell	**told**
write	**wrote**

I comparative (one syllable adjectives)

base form	**comparative**
big	**bigger**
small	**smaller**

Vocabulary

bigger	less	put (past tense)	than
blew out	lit	rang	told
city	made	said	took out
country	more	sat down	which
cover	mountain	smaller	wrote
hit (past tense)	one	state	
important	pitcher	surrounded	

PRONUNCIATION

Pronunciation Exercises

	A	B	C	D
1	sheep	ship		
2	net	nut	note	
3	cat	kite	coat	
4	wreck	rock	rake	
5	bucks	box	books	
6	cap	cup	cop	cape

Listen and Perform

Touch Put the coin on Point to the	the **ship.**

174

Pronunciation Exercises

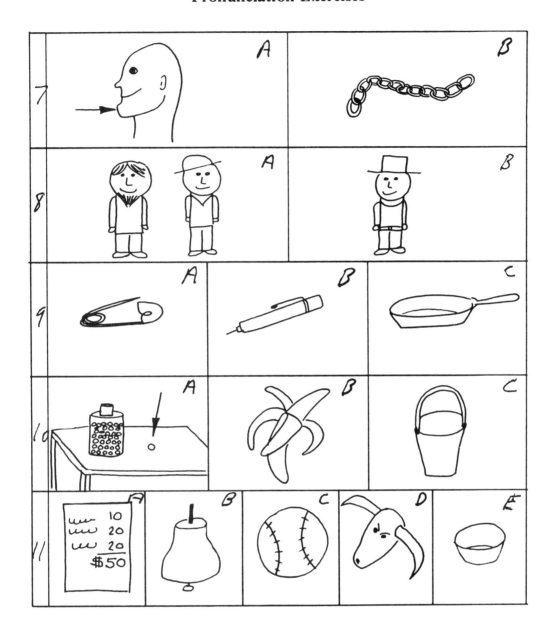

	A	B	C	D	E
7	chin	chain			
8	men	man			
9	pin	pen	pan		
10	pill	peel	pail		
11	bill	bell	ball	bull	bowl

Listen and Perform

Touch Put the coin on Point to	the **chin.**

Pronunciation Exercise

	A	B	C	D
12	thumb	sum	three	tree
13	king	kick	wing	wig
14	sum	sun		
15	rat	hat	ring	wing
16	rake	lake	hair	head

Listen and Perform

Touch Put the coin on Point to	the **thumb.**

Pronunciation Exercises

	A	B	C	D
17	teacher	T-shirt	chin	shin
18	jeep	sheep	year	cheer
19	year	ear	cheer	chair
20	peach	beach	cap	cab
21	ten	den	coat	code
22	coat	goat	back	bag

Listen and Perform

Touch Put the coin on Point to	the **chair.**

177

KEY TO THE EXERCISES

Lesson 1
Exercise 1
1. hands
2. jump
3. the
4. wave
5. down
6. to
7. it
8. with
9. him
10. turn

Key to the Exercises   **Lesson 1**
Exercise 2
1. Touch the chalkboard.
2. Everybody stand up.
3. Jump to the sofa.
4. Say "hello" to me.
5. Walk to the window.
6. Wave to a friend.
7. Whisper "good-bye" to the teacher.
8. Shake hands with a friend.
9. Walk to the sofa and sit down.
10. Jump to the window and touch it.

Lesson 2
Exercise 1
1. around
2. ceiling
3. then
4. places
5. hop
6. room
7. desk
8. run
9. who's
10. swim

Key to the Exercises   **Lesson 2**
Exercise 2
1. Touch the television.
2. Swim to the desk.
3. Point to the ceiling.
4. Run around the fan.
5. Hop to a wall.
6. Sit on the table.
7. Point to the chalkboard.
8. Jump around the class.
9. Change places with the teacher.
10. Shake hands with the teacher.

Lesson 3
Exercise 1
1. pretend
2. of
3. on
4. get
5. you're
6. back
7. next
8. an
9. in
10. to

Key to the Exercises   **Lesson 3**
Exercise 2
1. Now get down.
2. Pretend you're an airplane.
3. Point to the bird.
4. Pretend you're a chicken.
5. Everybody stand up.
6. Stand next to the chalkboard.
7. Who's in front of Fred?
8. Stand in back of the sofa.
9. Stand in front of the teacher.
10. Jump to the wall and touch it.

KEY TO THE EXERCISES

Lesson 4
Exercise 1
1. up the circle
2. to the triangle
3. window
4. the rectangle
5. d
6. down
7. it down
8. out of square
9. up
10. key to your friend

Key to the Exercises
Exercise 2
1. Pick it up.
2. Open the door.
3. Close the window.
4. Sit on a friend.
5. Pick up the triangle.
6. Put the square down.
7. Show it to the class.
8. Pretend you're an elephant.
9. Stand in back of a friend.
10. Give the book to the teacher.

Lesson 4

Lesson 5
Exercise 1
1. and pull my nose
2. say "cat" in Span.
3. me to the chalkb
4. the red fish
5. under the circle
6. friend's hair
7. ears; friend's hair
8. and the triangle
9. pull her nose
10. to an ear

Key to the Exercises
Exercise 2
1. Touch your ears.
2. Change places with me.
3. Pull a friend's hair.
4. Point to a friend's nose.
5. Put the triangle under the rectangle.
   Put the rectangle under the triangle.
6. Put the circle on the square.
   Put the square on the circle.
7. Touch the square and the triangle.
   Touch the triangle and the square.
8. Stand next to the desk and cry.
9. Pick up the key and open the door.
10. Stand in front of me and pull my nose.

Lesson 5

Lesson 6
Exercise 1
1. out
2. brother
3. happy
4. from
5. woman
6. sister
7. mother's
8. of
9. draw
10. chalk

Key to the Exercises
Exercise 2
1. Tell me your mother's name.
2. Give my sister the flower.
3. Now show your father the circle.
4. Take out a sheet of paper.
5. Write your name in the notebook.
6. Touch the man who's from Mexico.
7. Draw a happy face in a square.
8. Pick up the pencil and draw a circle.
9. Stand in front of me and touch my nose.
10. Take a triangle from Ted's desk and give it to me.

Lesson 6

179

KEY TO THE EXERCISES

Lesson 7
Exercise 1
1. your ear
2. nose and laugh
3. song by the beatles
4. us and pull our hair
5. under a big triangle
6. the floor
7. to someone
8. pulling your hair
9. a song
10. from Japan

Key to the Exercises   **Lesson 7**
Exercise 2
1. Hop around the table, singing.
2. Give your sister the flower.
3. Touch something on the desk.
4. Now show it to the class.
5. Sing a song by the beatles.
6. Pull a friend's ears and then cry.
7. Jump around the room, touching your nose.
8. Stand in front of us and pull our hair.
9. Walk to the window and close it.
10. Stand in back of the chair and point to the ceiling.

Lesson 8
Exercise 1
1. eyes
2. only
3. both
4. mouth
5. stoop
6. breathe
7. foot
8. tell
9. person
10. streth

Key to the Exercises   **Lesson 8**
Exercise 2
1. Close your mouth.
2. Point to both eyes.
3. Stoop next to the sofa.
4. Pull only one ear, not both.
5. Put your feet on the desk.
6. Put your hands on your ears.
7. How do you say "dog" in Spanish?
8. Draw a sad face with big eyes.
9. Give the triangle to the person who's sitting next to you.
10. Tell someone to cry and point to the person who's crying.

Lesson 9
Exercise 1
1. hat
2. them off
3. touch your shoulders
4. on the tie
5. on her chin
6. off
7. to your forehead
8. each cheek
9. the bracelet
10. who's wearing a cap

Key to the Exercises   **Lesson 9**
Exercise 2
1. Take it off.
2. Put on the tie.
3. Put down only the rectangle.
4. Touch the boy who's from England.
5. Touch the door with your nose.
6. Point to the boy who's wearing jeans.
7. Pick up both the square and the triangle.
   Pick up both the triangle and the square.
8. Draw a sad face with only one eye.
9. Tell two people to hop and point to them.
10. Pick up the circle but don't show it to me.

180

KEY TO THE EXERCISES

Lesson 10
Exercise 1

1. their
2. add
3. sum
4. without
5. times
6. shirt
7. after
8. between
9. count
10. wall

Key to the Exercises   **Lesson 10**
Exercise 2

1. Cough three times.
2. Add the numbers two and six.
   Add the numbers six and two.
3. Count the students in the class.
4. Draw a girl with a big nose.
5. Stand between the desk and the teacher.
   Stand between the teacher and the desk.
6. Draw a square next to the sum.
7. Write the number that comes after ten.
8. Touch the clock that's on the table.
9. Shake hands with a person who's wearing something red.
10. Stand in front of them and pull their hair.

Lesson 15
Exercise 1

1. can
2. wearing
3. wig
4. another
5. them
6. hold
7. head
8. fingers
9. some
10. earring

Key to the Exercises   **Lesson 15**
Exercise 2

1. Take them off.
2. Put on the wig.
3. Give me another pencil.
4. Draw some small flowers.
5. Shake the can five times.
6. Touch your head with one hand.
7. Draw a happy face with a beard.
8. Write the number that comes before seven.
9. Draw a fish with a heart on its head.
10. Touch the person who's sitting next to the desk.

Lesson 16
Exercise 1

1. in the purse
2. the other on the sofa
3. the candle
4. out
5. your pocket
6. out a match
7. showing five after six
8. smoking a cigarette
9. this?
10. box

Key to the Exercises   **Lesson 16**
Exercise 2

1. Light the candle.
2. Blow it out.
3. Show me your watch.
4. Put the matches in my purse.
   Put my matches in the purse.
5. Touch the circle that I'm touching.
6. Pull your hair with both hands.
7. Count the buttons on my brother's shirt.
8. Point to one circle and touch the other.
   Touch one circle and point to the other.
9. Draw a sad face wearing glasses and earrings. Draw a sad face wearing earrings and glasses.
10. Put a coin in the can and shake it.

KEY TO THE EXERCISES

Lesson 17
Exercise 1
1. make
2. isn't
3. sponge
4. with
5. half
6. squeeze
7. like
8. hand
9. into
10. lower

Key to the Exercises **Lesson 17**
Exercise 2
1. Make a paper airplane.
2. Squeeze a friend's nose.
3. Throw your mother the ball.
4. Throw the ball to a friend.
5. Draw a rectangle and divide it in half.
6. Fly the paper airplane to the window.
7. Throw the ball back to your friend.
8. Fly around the room like an airplane.
9. Hit me on the head with a book.
10. Write the name of someone who isn't here.

Lesson 18
Exercise 1
1. pour
2. dry
3. sleeping
4. own
5. pour
6. towel
7. bottom
8. curved
9. drink
10. center

Key to the Exercises **Lesson 18**
Exercise 2
1. Pretend you're sleeping.
2. Take out a match.
3. Show me your dry hand.
4. At the bottom, write your name.
5. Pour some water into the glass.
6. In the center, draw a sad face.
7. Pick up the towel and dry your hands.
8. Draw a curved line between two vertical line
   Draw a vertical line between two curved line
9. Now pour a little water on your own head.
10. Hold the glass while I pour some water into

Lesson 19
Exercise 1
1. shopping
2. something
3. of
4. jumped
5. showed
6. upper
7. there's
8. right
9. either
10. will

Key to the Exercises **Lesson 19**
Exercise 2
1. Ring the bell.
2. Raise your left hand.
3. Tell two people to cry.
4. Walk around the desk backwards.
5. Touch the chalkboard with an ear.
6. In the upper corners, draw a square.
7. Touch the four corners of this paper.
8. Draw a small cloud over a house.
   Draw a house over a small cloud.
9. Touch the girl who's flying a kite.
10. Pick up the triangle, but don't show it to me

KEY TO THE EXERCISES

Lesson 20
Exercise 1
1. shopping
2. something
3. of
4. jumped
5. showed
6. upper
7. there's
8. right
9. either
10. will

Key to the Exercises   **Lesson 20**
Exercise 2
1. Catch the ball.
2. Stand up and turn left.
3. Draw a butterfly between two clouds.
4. Write the name of a bank.
5. Draw a girl holding an umbrella.
6. I'm going to say a number.
7. If today's Monday, jump to the door.
8. Tell me the name of a beach.
9. Draw something you see at a supermarket.
10. In the lower left hand corner, draw a cat.

Lesson 21
Exercise 1
1. over
2. going to
3. upside-down
4. few
5. thin
6. whose
7. waved
8. this
9. star
10. many

Key to the Exercises   **Lesson 21**
Exercise 2
1. Draw many small circles.
2. Draw a few big triangles.
3. Draw three short vertical lines.
4. Draw a tall, thin man.
5. Hop to that student over there.
6. Touch the person you waved to.
7. Draw a fat man wearing a tie.
8. Draw a short man with a beard.
9. Draw an upside-down butterfly between two triangles.
10. Point to the person whose hair you pulled.

Lesson 22
Exercise 1
1. broken horizontal line
2. of the numbers you add
3. nose you pulled
4. you're facing
5. kicked
6. of water into the cup
7. cut your hair
8. through a heart
9. water into the pail
10. because he's short

Key to the Exercises   **Lesson 22**
Exercise 2
1. Raise both hands.
2. Shake your head two times.
3. Point to your wet hand.
4. Draw a long broken horizontal line.
5. Squeeze the sponge with both hands.
6. Draw an arrow through a fat man.
7. Pick up the scissors and cut my hair.
8. Pour a little bit of water into the cup.
9. Face a window and touch the window you're facing.
10. Draw a sad face with a triangle for its nose.

KEY TO THE EXERCISES

Lesson 23
Exercise 1
1. pray
2. upside-down
3. to
4. row
5. shelves
6. shelf
7. others
8. magazine
9. must
10. weren't

Key to the Exercises
Exercise 2
1. Kick the ball to me.
2. It must be Steve.
3. Draw seven hearts in a row.
4. Draw a clock above a desk.
   Draw a desk above a clock.
5. Sit on the sofa and pray.
6. Put the bowl on the table.
7. Open the magazine and read to me.
8. Tell me the name of a book.
9. He's going to jump to the window.
10. Draw a circle around one and a rectangle around the others.
    Draw a rectangle around one and a circle around the others.

Lesson 23

Lesson 24
Exercise 1
1. sang
2. drive
3. drew
4. threw
5. drank
6. ran
7. time
8. push
9. river
10. shook

Key to the Exercises
Exercise 2
1. Erase the circle you drew.
2. Push me to the chalkboard.
3. Pull your sister to the door.
4. Drive the car around the class.
5. Open the window you ran to.
6. It has to be your brother.
7. Draw two men swimming in a river.
8. Drop them on the floor one by one.
9. Touch the person you gave the flower to.
10. Tell me the name of the song you sang.

Lesson 24

Lesson 25
Exercise 1
1. "hello" to
2. that you made
3. who's hair you cut
4. you rang
5. match you took out
6. that you lit
7. sizes bigger
8. whose hair you cut
9. an important city
10. more than fifty

Key to the Exercises
Exercise 2
1. Blow out the match you lit.
2. Make the tall man's eyes bigger.
3. Touch the person who sat down.
4. Fly the paper airplane that you made.
5. Give me the paper you took out.
6. Touch the person whose hair you cut.
7. Touch the person who rang the bell.
8. Draw a rectangle around the name you wrote.
9. Point to the person you told to sit down.
10. Point to the person you hit on the head.

Lesson 25

WORD LIST

The **numbers refer to the lesson** in which the word first appears. Words that appear in the pronunciation are marked by the letter P.

a 1

above (prep) 23

across 24

add 10

a few 21

after (prep) 10

after (in time expressions) 16

after (sub conj) 19

again 17

against 15

air 17

airplane 3

airport 20

a little 18

a lot of 22

am 16

an 3

and 1

another 15

any 10

anything 24

are 3

aren't 8

arm 15

around (turn around) 1

around (around the desk) 2

arrow 22

at (throw at) 17

at (at the top) 18

back (n) 15

back (adv) 17

backwards 19

bag 16

ball 17

bank 20

be 22

beach 20

beard 15

because 22

before (prep) 10

before (sub conj) 19

bell 19

belly 15

below (prep) 23

between 5

big 7

bigger 25

bill P

bird 3

bit (= small amount) 22

black 5

blew out 25

blouse 7

blow out 16

blue 5

book 4

bookcase 23

both 8

bottle 17

bottle cap 24

bottom 18

bowl 22

box 16

boy 6

bracelet 9

Brazil 6

breathe in 8

breathe out 8

bridge 24

broken (line) 22

brother 6

brown 7

bucks P

bull P

but 2

butterfly 19

button (n) 10

button (v) 10

by (by the Beatles) 7

cab P

can (n) 15

candle 16

can't be 22

cap 9

cape P

car 24

cat 3

catch 17

ceiling 2

center 18

chain P

chair 1

chalk 6

chalkboard 1

change places 2

cheek 9

cheer P

chest 15

chicken 3

chin 9

sixty 23

skirt 7

sleep (v) 18

small 7

smaller 25

smoke (v) 16

sneeze 10

snore 18

so (conclusion) 19

sofa 1

some 15

someone 7

something 7

song 7

Spain 8

Spanish 5

sponge 17

square 4

squeeze 17

stand 3

stand up 1

star 21

state 25

stoop 8

stop 1

stretch 8

student 2

sum 10

sun 21

Sunday 19

supermarket 20

surrounded 25

swam 24

swim 2

table 2

take 6

take off 9

take out 6

tall 21

teacher 1

teeth 9

television 1

tell (= say) 6

tell (= order) 8

ten 10

than 25

that (dem pron) 2

that (rel pron) 8

that's rel pron) 8

the 1

theater 20

their 10

them 9

then (conclusion) 21

then (= next) 2

the other 16

watch (n) 9

water 18

wave 1

we 16

wear 7

Wednesday 19

week 19

we'll 20

were 21

we're 16

weren't 21

wet 18

what (qw) 16

what day (qw) 19

what's (qw) 16

what time (qw) 10

where (qw) 16

where's (qw) 16

which (qw) 25

while 18

whisper 1

whistle 7

white 5

who (qw) 2

who's (rel pron) 6

who's (qw) 2

whose (rel pron) 21

wig 15

will 20

window 1

wing P

with 1

without 10

woman 6

women 21

work 4

wreck P

write 6

wrote 25

year P

yellow 5

yes 2

yesterday 19

you 3

you'll 20

your 4

you're 3

INDEX

Expanded 4th Edition!
OUR BEST SELLER ! !

✓ Demonstrates step-by-step how to apply TPR to help children and adults acquire another language without stress.

✓ 150 hours of classroom-tested TPR lessons that can be adapted to teaching any language including Arabic, English, French, German, Hebrew, Japanese, Russian, Spanish, and the Sign Language of the Deaf.

Learning Another Language Through Actions

by

James J. Asher

Originator of the

World Famous

TOTAL PHYSICAL RESPONSE

Newly Expanded 4th Edition
Over 50,000 Copies in Print!

✓ Answers 175 of the most often asked questions about TPR.

✓ Explains why TPR works.

✓ Easy to understand summary of 20 years of research with James Asher's Total Physical Response.

✓ New chapter — TPR: A personal story is a behind-the-scenes look at how TPR was developed.

Practical Applications Of the Right-Left Brain

Brainswitching is a brand-new skill which you can use to move from one side of the brain to the other. This accelerates the mastery of "difficult" subjects such as foreign languages, mathematics, and science.

In this easy-to-read book, James Asher demonstrates with practical examples how you can use brainswitching to improve learning, problem solving, work, play, counseling, and interviewing.

After reading this book, you will have a clear picture of how the left and right brain works in processing information – and how you can use the skill of brain-switching to expand the potential for each of your students.

Triple Expanded 3rd Edition!

BEST-SELLER!!

For 20 years, Ramiro Garcia has successfully applied the Total Physical Response in his high school and adult language classes.

This Third Edition (300 pages) includes:

- Speaking, Reading, and Writing

- How to Create Your Own TPR Lessons.

Instructor's Notebook

How to Apply TPR For Best Results

By
RAMIRO GARCIA

Recipient of the
OUTSTANDING TEACHER AWARD

Edited by
James J. Asher

<u>And</u> more than 200 TPR scenarios for beginning and advanced students.

- TPR Games for all age groups.

- TPR Testing for all skills including oral proficiency.

In this illustrated book, Ramiro shares the tips and tricks that he has discovered in using TPR with hundreds of students. No matter what language you teach, including ESL and the sign language of the deaf, you will enjoy this insightful and humorous book.

The Graphics Book

For <u>All</u> Languages and Student of <u>All</u> Ages
by
Ramiro Garcia
edited by
James J. Asher

Dear Colleague:

You recall that I introduced graphics in the second edition of **Instructor's Notebook: How To Apply TPR For Best Results.** Hundreds of teachers tried the graphics with their students in many different languages including ESL and were excited to discover that the students of all ages thoroughly enjoyed working with the material.

Your students understand a huge chunk of the target language because you used TPR. Now, with my new graphics book, you can follow up with drawings on tear-out strips and sheets that help your students zoom ahead with more **vocabulary, grammar, talking, reading** and **writing** in the target language.

> # The Graphics Book
> ### For <u>All</u> Languages and Students of <u>All</u> Ages!
> *by*
> ## RAMIRO GARCIA
> *edited by*
> ## JAMES J. ASHER

In my book, you will receive easy–to-understand, step-by-step guidance in how to apply the graphics effectively with children or adults acquiring <u>any</u> language including ESL.

As an **extra bonus**, you will discover how to use the graphics to **test the achievement of your students** in comprehension, speaking, reading, and writing. In fact, I provide you with 60 graphic tests **for beginning and intermediate students.** Order **The Graphics Book** from Sky Oaks Productions in your choice of English, Spanish, French or German.

Best wishes for continued success,

Ramiro Garcia

Ramiro Garcia

TPR Bingo©

Sky Oaks Productions, Inc.
P.O. Box 1102
Los Gatos, CA 95031-1102

was created by Ramiro Garcia, author of the best-selling *Instructor's Notebook*. In 20 years of applying the Total Physical Response in his high school and adult Spanish classes, **TPR Bingo** is the game that students want to play over and over.

TPR Bingo has playboards for forty students. One side of a playboard has 9 pictures so that you can play **TPR Bingo** with beginning students and when the playboard is turned over, there are 16 pictures for bingo with advanced students.

Here's how **TPR Bingo** works: You call out a direction in the target language such as "The man opens the door." Students listen to the utterance, search for a matching picture and if it is on their playboard, cover it with a chip. You may order the game in *English, Spanish, French* or *German*.

When students listen to the instructor utter directions in the target language, they are *internalizing comprehension*. But, as they advance in understanding, individual students will ask to play the role of the caller which gives students valuable practice in *reading and speaking*. Incidentally, as students play **TPR Bingo**, they internalize numbers in the target language from 1 through 100.

As Ramiro says, "Try this game with your students. You will love it!"

Look, I Can Talk!

Student Textbook for Level 1
in English, Spanish, French or German
by Blaine Ray

Here is an effective **TPR** storytelling technique that **zooms** your students into *talking, reading,* and *writing.* It works beautifully with beginning, intermediate and yes, — even advanced students.

Step-by-step, Blaine Ray shows you how to tell a story with **physical actions**, then have your students *tell the story to each other* in their own words **using the target language**, then **act** it out, **write** it and **read** it.

Each **Student Textbook for Level 1** comes in your choice of *English, Spanish, French or German* and has

- ✔ 12 main stories
- ✔ 24 additional action-packed picture stories
- ✔ Many options for retelling each story
- ✔ Reading and writing exercises galore.

Blaine ***personally guarantees*** that each of your students will eagerly tell stories in the target language by using the **Student Textbook.**

To insure rapid student success, follow the thirteen magic steps explained in Blaine Ray's **Teacher's Guidebook** and then work with your students story-by-story with the easy-to-use **Overhead Transparencies.**

Look, I Can Talk <u>More!</u>

The Exciting Sequel! ## Student Textbook for Level 2

Order <u>now</u> in your choice of English, Spanish, or French!

Keep the excitement going with this sequel for your level 2 students. Ten main stories with many spin off mini-stories for variety. The drawings are superb and **Overhead Transparencies** may also be ordered. Your students will love it!

NEWS FLASH!

The popular TPR book, **Learning With Movements** by Nancy Márquez is available in **English, Spanish,** and now **French**.

The unique features are:

- A marvelously **simple format** which allows you to glance at a page and instantly generate one direction after another to move your students rapidly in a logical series of actions.

- An **initial screening test** will give you a realistic concept of each student's skill.

- After each lesson, there is a **competency test** for individual students.

- Recommended for beginning students of **all ages** and in **any language** including the sign language of the deaf.

NEW! In your choice of *English*, *Spanish*, or *French*!

Dear Colleague:

I want to share with you the **TPR Lessons** that my high school and college students have **thoroughly enjoyed** and **retained** for weeks—even months later. My book has

- A script you may follow step-by-step including a list of props needed to conduct each class.

- A command format that students thoroughly enjoy. (Students show their understanding of the spoken language by successfully carrying out the commands given to them by the instructor. **Production** is delayed until students are ready and feel comfortable.)

- Grammar taught implicitly through the imperative.

- Tests for an evaluation of student achievement.

Sincerely,

Francisco Cabello

FAVORITE GAMES *for* FL - ESL CLASSES

(For All Levels and All Languages)
by Margaret S. Woodruff-Wieding *and* Laura J. Ayala

PRIZE-WINNING TPR LESSONS

Here are **detailed lesson plans** for **60 hours** of **TPR Instruction** that make it **easy** for novice instructors to apply the **total physical response** approach **at any level.** The **TPR lessons** include

- **Step-by-step directions** so that instructors **in any foreign language** (including ESL) can apply comprehension training successfully.

- **Competency tests** to be given after the 10th and 30th lessons.

- **Pretested short exercises** — dozens of them to capture student interest.

- **Many photographs**

COMPREHENSION BASED LANGUAGE LESSONS

LEVEL 1

by

Margaret S. Woodruff, Ph.D.
Winner of the Paul Pimsleur Award
(With Dr. Janet King Swaffar)

Illustrations and photographs
by **Del Wieding**

NOTE!

Some people have requested the prize-winning lessons in English only, others wanted German only, and others wanted both German and English.

To satisfy everyone, we have printed the lessons in two languages — **English** and **German**, but we have charged you only the cost of printing a single language.

Hot New Book!

The Super School
Of The 21st Century
We Can Have It Now!
by James J. Asher, Ph.D.

Public education is under siege in California and most other states. Everyone is talking about alternative schools. Sounds promising—but realistically, what are our options?

Here is a blueprint for an alternative school that is so exciting, economical, and realistic that you will want your children and grandchildren to enroll now. It is packed with skills that prepare our young people, who will enter either white collar or blue collar occupations, to be super-competitive in the global markets of the 21st century where the secret of the "good life" is to work smarter, not harder.

James J. Asher, one of the most creative educational psychologists of our time (and recently honored as the Outstanding Professor of San José State University), demonstrates step-by-step how to make it happen in your community. The vision is spectacular—and when you finish the book, you will say: "Of course, this is the way to go! I knew it all along."

CLASSIC VIDEO DEMONSTRATIONS

Rental $29 each for first day and
$10 each additional day + S & H
Purchase: $95 each
U.S. Currency—*Prices subject to change without notice.*

CHILDREN LEARNING ANOTHER LANGUAGE: AN INNOVATIVE APPROACH

Written, Directed and Produced by James J. Asher

VHS • COLOR • 26 1/2 MINUTES • NARRATED IN ENGLISH

If you are searching for ways that motivate children to learn another language, don't miss this classic video demonstration. The ideas you will see can be applied in your classroom for **any grade level** and for **any language** including **English as a second language.**

This video shows children from kindergarden through the **6th grade**

- enjoying immediate understanding of everything the instructor is saying in **Spanish or French.**
- **keenly motivated** day after day.
- spontaneously making the transition from **understanding to speaking.**
- assimilating the target language in chunks rather than word by word.

The keen motivation and genuine achievement of these children will inspire teachers at all levels. You'll want to see this video two or three times to pick up the subtle details.

CLASSIC VIDEO DEMONSTRATIONS

Rental $29 each for first day and
$10 each additional day + S & H
Purchase: $95 each
U.S. Currency—*Prices subject to change without notice.*

A MOTIVATIONAL STRATEGY FOR LANGUAGE LEARNING

Written, Directed and Produced by James J. Asher

VHS • COLOR • 26 MINUTES • NARRATED IN ENGLISH

How can students be motivated to continue in a language program year after year?

In this classic video demonstration you will see the excitement as **adults from 17 to 60** understand everything the instructor is saying in Spanish. The technique is to direct the students through commands, which is the essence of TPR training. As you watch, notice the rich grammatical structure which can be communicated through the imperative.

After several weeks in which the students are silent, but responding rapidly to commands in Spanish, there comes a time when the students are spontaneously **ready to talk.** You will see this interesting transition from **understanding to speaking.**

Next, you will see the **transfer-of-learning to reading and writ**ing. Once students could understand everything the instructor was saying in Spanish, they could immediately read.

Finally, you will **witness the creativity of students** as they invent and act out skits. All the student skits are superb, but the Santa Claus scene may be a classic in the genre of student inventions. Everything you will see was filmed the first year of an experimental TPR course.

CLASSIC VIDEO DEMONSTRATIONS

Rental $29 each for first day and
$10 each additional day + S & H
Purchase: $95 each
U.S. Currency—*Prices subject to change without notice.*

STRATEGY FOR
SECOND LANGUAGE LEARNING
Written, Directed and Produced by James J. Asher

VHS • COLOR • 22 MINUTES • NARRATED IN ENGLISH

Students can enjoy the thrill of achieving basic fluency in another language if they remain in a program long enough. The problem is that most students "give up" too soon.

This video demonstration presents one solution based on a TPR model of infants learning their first language. You will see **adults of all ages** understanding German when the instructor directs their behavior by uttering commands. You will be surprised at the complexity of grammatical structure that can be nested in the imperative.

Even when the class meets only two nights a week and no homework is required, the retention of spoken German is impressive. Then, after a few weeks in which the students silently act out directions in German, there is a **readiness to talk.** At this point, you will see **role reversal** in which the students enthusiastically utter directions in German to move the instructor about the room.

You will be impressed by the graceful transition from **understanding to reading and writing.** And you will enjoy the creativity shown by students as they invent and act out problems.

You will see in 60 seconds with time lapse photography, one student's progress through the entire course from zero understanding of German to conversational skill.

This video has been used at the University of Texas at Austin to orient and **motivate hundreds of students** who enrolled in language programs.

CLASSIC VIDEO DEMONSTRATIONS

Rental $29 each for first day and
$10 each additional day + S & H
Purchase: $95 each
U.S. Currency—*Prices subject to change without notice.*

DEMONSTRATION OF A NEW STRATEGY IN LANGUAGE LEARNING

Written, Directed and Produced by James J. Asher

VHS • BLACK & WHITE • 19 MINUTES • NARRATED IN ENGLISH

You will see the first demonstration of the **Total Physical Response** ever recorded on film when American children **rapidly internalize** a complex sample of Japanese. Step-by-step you will also see the **astonishing retention one year** after the experiment. Narrated by the originator of TPR, James J. Asher.

This classic film has been seen by thousands of language teachers, linguists, and psychologists in the U.S.A. and other countries.

NOTE:
These video demonstrations have been used with success in hundreds of universities, high schools, and grammar schools throughout the world—from the Bilingual Education Center of Bethel Alaska to Cambridge University in England... from the Chinatown Resources Development Center in San Francisco to the Sakura no Seibo Junior College in Japan... from Stanford University in California to New York University.

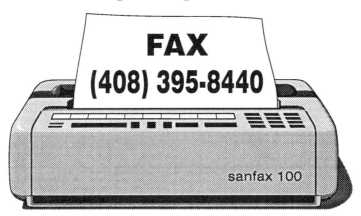